Prentice-Hall, Inc., Englewood Cliffs, New Jersey 07632   A SPECTRUM BOOK

S0-AJE-220

VIDEO/ COMPUTERS

How to Select, Mix, and Operate Personal Computers and Home Video Systems

Charles J. Sippl and Fred Dahl

Library of Congress Cataloging in Publication Data

Sippl, Charles J
   Video computers.

   (A Spectrum Book)
   Includes index.
   1. Computer terminals—Interactive terminals.
2. Microcomputers.   3. Data transmission systems.
4. Television display systems.   I. Dahl, Fred, joint
author. II. Title.
TK7887.8.T4S57   621.3819'532   81-26
ISBN 0-13-941856-3
ISBN 0-13-941849-0 (pbk.)

Editorial/production supervision by Fred Dahl
Interior design by Christine Gehring Wolf
Manufacturing buyer: Barbara Frick

© 1981 by Prentice-Hall, Inc., Englewood Cliffs, New Jersey 07632

A SPECTRUM BOOK

10 9 8 7 6 5 4 3 2 1

Printed in the United States of America

Prentice-Hall International, Inc., *London*
Prentice-Hall of Australia Pty. Limited, *Sydney*
Prentice-Hall of Canada, Ltd., *Toronto*
Prentice-Hall of India Private Limited, *New Delhi*
Prentice-Hall of Japan, Inc., *Tokyo*
Prentice-Hall of Southeast Asia Pte. Ltd., *Singapore*
Whitehall Books Limited, *Wellington, New Zealand*

Contents

3

4

5

6

Preface

Practically every American household contains video and audio terminals right now—the television and telephone. Home computer hobbyists also have processing centers, and those with modems or acoustic couplers even have digital communication capability. As more and more personal computers are sold, the need for integrating all this household hardware becomes greater and greater. Thus the video, computer, and communications industries come to a common, pinpoint focus in the home—in the form of the integrated video computer (IVT).

All over the country, and indeed all over the world, the IVT concept is materializing out the greater-than-ever need for eye-blinking fast, dot-the-eye accuracy in communications today. As a sterling example, in November of 1980, the French Pavilion at the Intelcom 80 show presented a range of products called "Telematique Programme." As advertised, it is "a new telephone system that isn't all talk." The proposed Telematique terminal combines a CRT screen, keyboard, and phone transceiver. The dial buttons are part of a larger keyboard, which can be used for placing calls or for inputting data. The screen can be used either for processing output or for display of visual messages received from other terminals. The system will also make available to users such services as teleshopping, automated reservations, electronic mail, and access to a wide range of databases. The system is due for a $30-million, quarter-million-terminal trial throughout 1981.

In the same month of the same year, *Time* magazine led off an article, entitled "Now the Office of Tomorrow," with these words:

> In Stamford Conn., and Palo Alto, Calif., two secretaries of the Xerox Corp. use electronic mail computers to swap and file memos from their bosses, thereby reducing to a minute's time a chore that previously would have involved typing letters and sending them coast to coast.

Ultimately, these developments in business and elsewhere will come to bear on the video and computer systems in the home—everyone's home. These two types of systems have been, up to now, only superficially "integrated." A manufacturer might install a chip in a video player/recorder for greater automation, or a video game maker might put a modulator between its computer/game and the home TV set. By the end of this decade, however, *real* integration must of necessity take its place in the home.

Between then and now, the remaining years of the decade could prove to be most exciting for those who have eyes to see.

With this inevitability in mind, we have composed this book in such a way as to anticipate, as much as possible, the trends in this direction. In so doing, we have asked—and answered as far as we can—some basic questions: Which communications medium—conventional phone lines, fiber optic cables, satellites—will become the medium of the future? Is the standard home television set adequate for IVT applications? Is the IVT going to be fundamentally an analog or digital system? What functions might be reasonably expected of the integrated system?

In trying to work out answers to such questions, you quickly run into a tangled mess. So each chapter attempts to view the issues from a different viewpoint.

Chapter 1, "The Integrated Video Terminal," poses the scenario of future IVT applications in the home—working for an employer while never leaving your home, paying bills without writing out checks, ordering groceries without going shopping, writing a friend electronically, and a number of other capabilities. This chapter also itemizes and discusses the forces that are bringing about the public acceptance of these ideas.

Chapter 2, "The Video Enthusiast's Point of View," explains the video transmission and reception potential of the IVT, in light of the current standard broadcasting specifications. It also deals with the contributions of fast- and slow-scan IVT communications.

Chapter 3, "The Computerist's Point of View," delves into the essential conflicts between the digital nature of computer processing and the analog requirements of video equipment.

Chapter 4, "The IVT Configuration," discusses the system's problems and great potential. This chapter combines the conclusions of the prior two chapters to suggest several possible configurations.

Chapter 5, "The Communicator's Point of View," takes a step beyond the hardware. Assuming that the IVT terminal becomes a common enough piece of hardware in the home, the next question is how does one such terminal communicate with another?

Chapter 6, "Public Acceptance," is an extremely short chapter that can go only so far because it deals with such an intangible factor. Standing at the technological "edge of the earth," you can only guess at what is over the horizon.

Whether you are a video buff or computer hobbyist, we hope that our efforts will help you orient your interests to the exciting developments of the years to come.

CHARLES J. SIPPL
FRED DAHL

chapter **1**

The Integrated
Video Terminal

Sometime in the
Not-So-Distant Future

You turn on your home television set. But instead of lounging in an overstuffed sofa across the room, you are seated on a wheeled office chair directly in front of it. And the set, instead of blinking on with the latest spin-off sitcom, flashes a large, block-lettered "YES?" and, in smaller letters, "MAY I HELP YOU?"

Putting down your morning coffee, you touch a few of the keys on the typewriter-like keyboard in front of you. The keys do not move; just the touch of your fingertips activates the corresponding response. Deftly, you type, "PUNCHING IN," and the current time appears in the upper left-hand corner of the screen, followed by a picture of your boss, who is smiling.

"Good morning," you say. "Just punching in."

"Good morning. I'm glad you're a little early. We have a full day of assignments, and the section head has called a meeting for two this afternoon." He smiles again and nods goodbye.

A nanosecond or two later, his image is gone, and in its place you see a listing of your work for the day. As you instruct your computer terminal to "read" them into storage, the lines march one by one off the bottom of the screen. When the last one disappears, you know you're ready to start your day's work, which will be monitored by your employer's main computer 150 miles away in the city.

At lunchtime, after checking out from work, you decide to write a letter to a friend in Europe, who, of course, owns the same sort of terminal as yours (but one of those older models). As you key in your letter, the words and paragraphs appear on the screen before you. Finished, you scroll it back and forth to see what you've said. Deciding not to tell your friend yet about the possibility of changing jobs, you press a button to delete the paragraph. Satisfied with the contents, you send it off to Europe by routing it through the modem. The letter is off through the phone lines and satellite networks, on its way to Europe. At its destination, it will gain access to your friend's terminal by electronically giving it the owner's "computer address." Once your friend's terminal admits the message, the letter goes into storage there until the owner "checks the mail." If he wishes, he can just read the message off the screen or have it printed onto a hard copy. In the meantime, of course, you've kept an electronic "copy" on file in your terminal's storage.

After dispatching the letter, you have just enough time to do some of the household books. By accessing your bank account from the bank's computer, you make sure that your employer has credited your account with the proper after-tax amount for the week. (The company has also credited the fiduciary account at the bank for your withholding and FICA obligations.) Still in touch with the bank computer, you instruct it through your terminal to credit, "Utilities, Inc.—$75.32—ID# 1234567890." That's one bill paid. (You thank heaven for having the foresight years ago to install solar panels and a windmill to generate most of your own electricity. With the home computer in control of the sensors—turning the panels toward the sun, rotating the windmill into the wind, switching the heat on or off depending on temperature, and so on—you pay only 10 percent of what others pay for utilities.)

Lunch is over, and you go back to work. With your assignments only partially completed, you have to relegate those that remain undone to the next day's tasks, since the boss is calling an employees' meeting right away. You wait only a few seconds before the boss' face is again on the screen, explaining the need for promptness in reporting snags in assignments. He is taking suggestions on solving the problem, and, as each attendee speaks, his or her face appears on the screen. This aspect of employee meetings makes you self-conscious about the micro-camera—no bigger than a matchbox—in the housing of the terminal that is geared to switch you "onto the floor" when you press the talk button directly underneath it. Even though you do not press the button, you have the secret feeling that it is watching you anyway, as you ease back in your chair and listen halfheartedly with your eyes closed. The end of the meeting coincides with the end of the work day, so everyone is dismissed. You punch out.

On the "way home from work," you access the supermarket computer and order a delivery of groceries. A small order, just enough to hold you until you can figure out what you need for the upcoming week. The clerk at the computer verifies the order, and you sign off the total to the bank computer, which instantaneously deducts the amount from your account.

figure 1-1   Teletext provides access to hundreds of "pages" of information—news, weather, advertising, and more. This woman calls out the information by means of the hand-held terminal. Access to data bases through video channels is a feature of a number of cable and broadcasting networks today.

As you do some household chores, you insert the user-recordable videodisc, which you used to record the ballgame being telecast while you were working. You view about a half-hour of the game before having to turn it off. You hope you don't hear the final score on the radio before seeing the rest of the game.

Then you take off for an hour of tennis before dinner. This time has become available to you in the past few years, since you no longer have to spend a couple of hours each day traveling to and from work.

When you get back, the order should be delivered, you can make dinner, then perhaps catch the start of the new PBS science series . . .

Working without commuting . . . electronic mail . . . electronic funds transfer . . . teleshopping . . . time-shifted televiewing . . . these and many other capabilities of the future's scenario are all within the boundaries of today's technology! You could have all these features at your fingertips right now, if technology were the only source of delay.

4

What's Happening
In Computers and
Office Equipment?

The technology of the electronics and computer industries keeps drawing wonders from the air, like a good fairy with a magic wand that has run amuck. It can't help producing one marvel after another. As we shall see, the few technical barriers to having such a terminal in everyone's home are quickly crumbling under the scientific magic of engineers, designers, and tinkerers all over the world. In such a heady atmosphere, observers have a hard time not becoming rapturously prophetic of new Utopias.

Even the more hard-nosed spectators have to admit, however, that the time for such marvels is approaching. For example, a 1980 survey of the 400 leading designers/manufacturers of computers and office equipment led the Technology and Communications Editor of *Business Week* to believe that by 1985:

- employees in many fields will do their office work at a computer terminal in their own homes;
- executives will hold international conferences via satellite, without leaving their offices;
- secretaries, so indispensable today, will be largely replaced by desk-top computers; and
- medium to large companies will have electronic information networks that use space satellites to interconnect computer and word processors at local plants and offices.

THE HARDWARE FOR A
REVOLUTION

Indeed, events in all sections of our society seem to bear out these predictions. Business persons, professionals, and "home computerists" all over the world are equipping themselves with the necessary terminal hardware. For example, Montgomery Ward has installed roughly 19,000 terminals in its organization; Bank of America, 12,000; and many large firms average 10,000 to 20,000. In France, approximately 10,000 microterminals have been installed throughout the school system. The British government has allocated $20 million for the installation of microterminals throughout its school system in the early eighties. Apparently doctors in the United States are so wrapped up with their personal computers that some of them are issuing the *Physicians Microcomputer Report.* Even the so-called "hobbyists"—who are quickly blending with the general population as microcomputer owners—purchased 100,000 of Radio Shack's TRS-80s in 1978 alone and turned Apple Computer Company into a multimillion-dollar business from a garage based operation in just three years.

Even the larger, traditionally staid manufacturing firms are promoting communications hardware. IBM, perhaps the best example of a giant in a marketplace filled with bustling pygmies, is promoting its Model 6670 Information Distributor at $75,000: It is capable of telecopying information from one coast to the other in 15 seconds. It even reduces computer printouts to letter size, prints on both sides of a sheet, and changes typestyles within a page. Xerox offers a similar service that is compatible with any make telecopier and that transmits hard copies at 16 cents a minute. Qwip is a desk-top fax machine that looks like a typewriter but that telecommunicates up to 15 pages or receives up to 150 pages of copy automatically during regular or off-business hours. It can be rented for as little as $50 a month.

The demand for terminals is so great that even the nation's telephone companies feel compelled to get into the scramble. By 1980, Continental Telephone, the fourth largest phone firm in the country, bought a major communications network, while in the same year Rochester Telephone was selling terminals, and United Telephone was heavily involved in computer services. The race was on.

Why such a sudden and dramatic demand for these terminals? The by-now well known reason is that microelectronics is making these desk-top computers capable of handling computer-oriented tasks on a "distributed" basis. In other words, no longer do users have to slave at "dumb" terminals just to gain access to a central Behemoth computer, which handles hundreds or thousands of requests and which stops the whole show when it breaks down. Nowadays, intelligent terminals sprinkled throughout an organization handle workloads on a distributed basis, each doing its own tasks without a great regard for what the others are doing and without dependence on a central processor. A breakdown on one does not hold up the others. And they are far simpler to use than any of the earlier, larger computers; they are truly user-oriented.

Even more exciting is that this market is just starting to open up. The aim of all computer producers is a "Computer in Every Home," yet they haven't even scratched the surface, especially in the business world. In 1979, Booz, Allen & Hamilton estimated that the "new" office equipment market would represent billions in sales annually. In dollars, that figure begins to approach the oil market. Most (in fact, about 80 percent) of this buying power is represented not by the large Fortune 500 firms but rather by small- to medium-sized companies who exercise great caution in making their purchases. Since office expenditures are historically only a tenth of corresponding expenditures in manufacturing, researchers everywhere believe that this "young" market has a lot of growing and buying to do.

These terminals, however, are only one aspect of an overall trend toward the consolidation of equipment and tasks in the business office today. Office machines are considered old-fashioned unless they can perform more than one function. In this respect, office devices, and their concomitant functions, are undergoing an integrating trend—telephones, copiers, typewriters, filing systems, and so on. The latest office copier models, for instance, just don't sell unless they are intelligent enough to offer facsimile printing, transmission, storage, and other features. In fact, the latest models are becoming "document distributors."

Telephones too are quickly expanding their role as voice communicators; nowadays PBX-systems are becoming integrated with data processing and data communications networks. As a "for-instance," the Alpex 900 not only takes messages, unattended, on either the screen or the printer, but it also acts as a computer terminal. In competition with the phone networks, packet switching networks offer such services as formatting, storage, and moving information, as well as data computation and distribution.

And the typewriter is no longer just a typewriter. The Basic Office Machine microcomputerized portable typewriter may look like a typewriter, but it is actually a consumer-priced word-processor with a spelling dictionary and daisy-wheel-like print-er. And the Qyx, as another example, also looks a lot like a typewriter, but it too is a combination of intelligent typewriter, WP terminal, and DP communications terminal. The Lanier No Problem word processor calls itself a "typewriter" (that's the way it's advertised), and yet it looks like a typewriter keyboard hooked up to a TV set. Stepping even farther away from the original concept of the typewriter is the Vydec 2000 word processor. This system is actually a WP terminal with mass storage, a keyboard, display, and communications capability. The point is, why mess around with ink on paper when you can get it locked in forever—electronically—and reproduce or trans-mit it as needed?

What's happening is that all the traditional office ma-chines, now taking up space on the desk, are being gathered up into more and more integrated devices. They're all gradually becoming housed in the same make-believe wood grain cabi-nets. In the early eighties, for example, Exxon Enterprises, was working on an "integrated electronic office network" designed so as to consolidate filing, database management, data storage accessing, work processing, electronic mail, voice communi-cations, and other standard office and computer functions.

Yet Exxon is only a titan in a long parade that is led by a small firm called Ql Corporation. This firm, with a record of firsts in microsystem design, markets the Basic Office Machine, which in 1980 was a word processor, general purpose desk-top computer, typewriter, electronic data storage device, and com-municator. Ql plans to make the BOM much more flexible and versatile in the future, adding copy and telecopying, scanning, and other functions. Its aim is to make its product the *only* office machine that any office needs.

Of course, these companies are not alone. Other electronic product manufacturers—including the makers of video equip-ment—are in no way blind to this revolution. In fact, they foster it in every way they can. The makers of TV games, home computers, video recorder/players, and the like—the personal electronics industry—are headed straight for the "home" mar-ket. The popularity of each year's crop of new electronic devices attests to the public's eagerness to try out new gadgets. So the phenomenon taking place in business merely parallels what is happening in the personal electronics market.

This leaning toward integration and consolidation, as well as the clamor for newer and better gadgetry, reflects a world that is rapidly equipping itself on all levels—at home, in offices, in schools, throughout government offices and the military. Like nerve synapses in a living organism, these terminal/computers are peppered all over the globe.

And like nerve centers, they are extending neurons toward one another, growing networks for communication. Listen to just a partial list of satellite and groundline networks:

- AT&T's Advanced Communications Service (ACS), a predecessor of its Antelope system due in 1983.
- Bell Telephone's Gemini 10, an electronic blackboard that transmits a person's handwriting to remote stations, as the sender writes on the board.
- Datapoint's Lightlink, an optical transmission network.
- General Telephone & Electronic's TELENET, a data transmission packet network.
- IBM/AMI's proposed electronic mail system via satellite that promises to send a copy a second.
- ITT's FAXPAK, a facsimile-transmitting system that costs as low as 20 cents a minute.
- MicroNET and SOURCE, the two most popular personal computer networks.
- Microwave Communications, Inc. (MCI)'s Super Network Discount for low-cost long-distance communications.
- PCNet NOVATION are others of dozens of personal computer networks.
- RCA's Q-fax that will telecopy pages at $8 a sheet anywhere in the world.
- Southern Pacific Communications' Sprint V long-distance phone communications system.
- TYMNET, an electronic mail transfer that uses computer terminals and facsimile terminals.
- UPI's installation of small, roof-top receiving antennas at the sites of its customers, for quicker distribution of news information via satellite.
- Wang's Mailway, an electronic mail system.
- Xerox's Ethernet, a single coax cable throughout an office building for the exclusive use of computers.

These networks are not just on the drawing board. They are here, and they are being used this very moment. As just a few examples of what's happening in communications, consider   *9* that the world's first all-automatic, electronic mail system went into operation in the spring of 1979 between Toronto and Montreal. Called Fascan, it is the brainchild of Bell Canada and Kaye & Associates, Inc. of Toronto. The charges were 98 cents for two-hour service, $1.35 for express 15-minute service, and 70 cents for overnight "delivery." By mid-year, the system was spreading to Vancouver, Calgary, and Ottawa. In the same vein, Exxon executives regularly hold teleconferences involving representatives from the company's offices in Houston, New York, Calgary, and Toronto. And Crown Zellerbach Paper offices use Bell Telephone's teleconferencing services, coast to coast, for less than $400. Highly paid executives, whose time can be worth hundreds of dollars *an hour*, regularly save days' and weeks' worth of traveling time each year by teleconferencing and other forms of electronic communication.

And if you think that electronic communications is something for the business world, think again: By the early eighties, industry leaders expect to market *personal* receive-only satellite antennas for mounting on home rooftops for a cost that is anticipated to be under $1,000. Representatives of Japanese manufacturers', in their typical take-it-and-do-better approach, feel they can produce these antennas for under $500. Is this amount such a large expenditure for those who perhaps have accumulated several thousands of dollars worth of computer equipment already?

What's Happening In TV Land?

What's true for the world of computers and office equipment is true for the world of video equipment and communications. For everyone who has paid to put up with the amoebic shuffling of the United Post Office, another one gags on the sitcoms, spinoffs, soaps, and game shows, all of which have the consistency of intellectual baby food: These bottom-of-the line selections are broadly transmitted at specific hours to the masses. For better or worse, you can take 'em or leave 'em. This is American commercial TV. People are ready for changes in both worlds. Too many unsavory mind-grinding programs are offered by a tight circle of "selectors," on profit-motivated stations.

NARROWCASTING

Most programs that are worth sitting through the commercials for are usually scheduled to run at the same time as head-on competition. The viewer is then forced to anguish over a choice, and good shows are often lost to the viewer forever. This type of entertainment definitely makes it tough on the consumer. Millions of consumers have complained that only at very few times during the year is a commercial-loaded TV program worthy of an hour or two of watching. Many critics suggest that the really good shows of the year can usually be counted on the fingers of one hand. These people turn to pay TV, to public television, and to cable TV (CATV) for more entertaining programming. Narrowcasting, in its various forms, is a concept-come-true: A switch on the term "broadcasting," it is the specific selection and copying of normally broadcast programming; it can also describe the payment for narrowcasts now offered by pay TV, as well as the purchase of educational videodiscs. Narrowcasting gifts consumers with complete control over what they want to watch, along with the freedom to do so when it is personally convenient.

VIDEO RECORDING

For every viewer who craves more special interest programs, another—at least according to the many rating agencies—is quite content with the present programming, doesn't want to miss any of the favorites, and often desperately wants to preserve many of them in collectors' libraries. These are the buyers of video equipment. For a large number of people, TV comprises a major share of their lives. Surveys of buyers of videocassette recorder/players (VCRs) show that many people with incomes as low as $10,000 a year save diligently to be able to purchase the equipment necessary to expand and enhance this share.

Such is their eagerness to buy that media rooms have suddenly become a vogue. People are converting dens, family rooms, home offices, and other facilities into personal communication centers. These rooms contain videocassette recorder/players, videodisc players, home CB base stations, stereo systems, various programmable TV and other electronic games, TV projection systems, home computers, and other media devices and systems.

Two-way is the future of TV; participatory television offers viewers the use of calculator-like terminals to answer the originating station—voting on the current program, participating with studio audiences in games, questioning interviewees, and so on. The videocassette recording of programs on some systems from a selection of thirty channels gives CATV great promise.

TELETEXT

Essentially, teletext is communication of the "selected" written word by means of a television screen instead of the printed page. Just as an author or news reporter types out a story and passes it on for publishing—typesetting, camera work, plating, printing, binding, shipping, sales—the teletext system brings the message directly from the hands of the author to the viewer. The author prepares the information in such a way so as to be accepted into a central database in which all such information is compiled. Even though it has to go through the hands of a professional data processor, the information is available within hours of its coming into being—as opposed to days, weeks, or months according to printed publication schedules. The information, once entered into the central database, is immediately and selectively available for anyone who subscribes to the system, by using the calculator-like hand-held terminal, either through the phone lines or over the air waves.

Viewdata. By far the boldest experiment along these lines is Viewdata, a pilot database program, started up in January of 1976 by the British Post Office. By mid-1981 this upstart idea was ready to take over the world by offering to every individual who owns a television set instant access to just about any kind of information you can think of—from the best places to eat to the latest legislation from Congress, Parliament, the Diet—all displayed in seven bright colors.

Viewdata is a two-way information dissemination system by which the end consumer—the person normally sitting bleary-eyed in front of the TV set—is given access to many a huge database of information. The system utilizes a standard television, existing phone lines, and information from an ever growing database. The only purchase on the consumer's part is for a portable terminal with a keypad and decoder unit, which either hooks up to the TV or is built into it.

The information can be about anything—from the best eating places in town to whether the user can adopt a child. The information is fed into the databases, according to specifications laid down by the British Post Office, by anyone who wants to contribute—from both the private and the public sector. Suppliers of information are paid according to the amount of usage by the consumer. The cost to the consumer, depending on the source of the information sought, could range from nothing to several dollars per selection.

In Canada, the system is called Telidon, and the terminal may be used as a home computer, for electronic mail, and for similar applications. Both the hardware and the software are designed for future improvements. The terminal would cost about $500. Field testing involves cable, phone, dedicated wire, and optical-fiber transmission.

With the portable terminal, containing the microprocessor and special electronics, the viewer can access information in one of three ways:

1. *Directly.* If the exact page number of the information is known, the user simply punches the numbers out on the terminal's keypad, and the page appears.
2. *By subject category.* If the viewer is searching for information by subject, he or she must start with general key terms and work downwards to smaller and smaller subsegments of the subject category until the particular information is on the screen.
3. *Interactively.* If the user has a particular question that cannot be answered with a simple submission of information, he or she may interact with the database to search out an answer. For instance, viewers might want to know whether they are eligible for workmen's compensation. They would interact with the database as though flipping through the pages of a book.

Since printers are obviously desirable for the making of hard copies of the screen image, several Japanese and American companies offered them in late 1979. Some two thousand were made up by hobbyists in England, and by 1980 the managers of U.S., French, Canadian, German, and other enterprises were planning on the production of suitable printers.   *13*

Purchasing by Barclay and other bank cards through Viewdata was in the works, as were built-in videogames and home computer services.

This growing interest was kindled by the British, stoked by the French Telematique system. Both laid the plans and allocated the funds for world-wide pushes in 1981. The initial pilot program had every earmark of success in Great Britain, and database enlargement programs and expanded services were running according to plans. The system software had been sold to the German Bundespost, and negotiations were then in progress with Hong Kong, Scandinavia, the Benelux, and the Latin countries. Viewdata (now called "Prestel" in the U.K.) was on the move. Fifteen million Britons were expected to be customers in the early 1980s.

Viewdata is here, and it is growing. Every day more databases become larger, more up-to-date. Every day a few more people buy the little terminal and pay the rate for the service. Every day more businesses decide that some portion of the database could be of assistance in conducting business.

Qube. Qube is another domestic two-way system—one of many starting up in this country. For several years now, residents of Columbus, Ohio, have been participating in a different kind of cable TV. Approximately 100,000 city residents have been offered hand-held terminals that enable them to interact with their cable TVs in some ways different from the British or French systems. Unlike those systems, however, the emphasis seems to be more on entertainment and participatory television viewing.

For a small initial fee, Warner Cable, a subsidiary of Warner Communications installs cable TV in the resident's home, with the usual benefits of pay TV. For a bit more a month, the viewer also gets a small terminal hooked into the set, a device that opens the door to many exciting experiences, such as:

1. *Interactive television*—voting and immediate tabulation on game shows.
2. *News read-outs*—on two channels, when you want them.
3. *Specialized programming*—for the children or of a religious nature.
4. *Billing and ordering*—through the TV station's computer.
5. *Exclusive programming*—shows that will "appear" only on specially authorized sets.
6. *Home security*—by means of a link to the city's police department.

The Qube system, as it is called, is a multi-million dollar experiment by Warner Cable. Like the British, Warner is pushing to exploit its newfound service. In late 1979, it built additional installations in Houston and suburban Cincinnati, and it applied for permission to build in Pittsburgh. About the same time, American Express agreed to acquire 50 percent of Warner Communications for $175 million in cash and short-term notes. If the gamble pays off, it could be a precursor of a whole new kind of television across the country. Columbus is only one out of 138 cable systems owned and operated by Warner throughout the United States.

Other Systems.   Teletext systems are catching the interest of more and more business leaders all over the world. Canada, France, and Japan have similar even more far-ranging systems: Videofax, Antiope, and combinations with cable systems in Japan. Still another system began in Japan in 1978. Though consisting of only three hundred subscribers, it works just like the other systems and offers: special programming, data on special request, computer-aided instruction, cashless transactions, TV shopping and reservations and a security capability.

In America in June of 1979, General Telephone and Electronics obtained licenses allowing it to offer Viewdata in the U.S. and Canada. At the same time, RCA, Motorola, and Western Union were all reported to be testing the system, even if only on a limited basis. And Bell Labs offers Viewtron in Coral Gables, Florida, a system by which users can teleshop at Grand Union supermarkets, buy travel reservations, get the latest news from Associated Press, procure educational services, among many other things. A firm in the United Kingdom, called Technologics Ltd., offers TECS (Technologics Expandable Computer System). It provides Viewdata, Teletext, and color computing facilities in a single desktop unit. It is designed with a standard domestic television set that can be used as a Viewdata editing terminal. A wide variety of peripherals can be attached. The system was available in kit form for less than $2000 or completely assembled for approximately $2300.

By the end of the eighties, we could very likely be looking back at the television of today with mock nostalgia. Remember when you had to wait for the news? Remember when you had to keep twenty or thirty books on your shelf to be able to look up   *15* information—information that was largely stale by the time it was printed anyway? Remember when you actually had to write out a check and mail it in to the department store to order something? Remember when you had to read a book to learn about the latest developments in computer technology?

Once enough people are hooked into such a system to spread the costs, the limitations on the applications are beyond view. Rendered obsolete, sooner or later, will be newspapers and news magazines, directories, catalogs, encyclopedias, newsletters, many magazines, much print advertising, among many, many other items. Such is the potential effect of teletext applications (Table 1–1).

The only question seems to be how soon the various systems will "catch on." They will—if the owners of Viewdata and a dozen other similar services have anything to say about it. Like any new idea—especially one of such a revolutionary and far-reaching nature—early Viewdata managers had an uphill push to get people to try the system. However, very soon worldwide competition set in and many systems became familiar enough to the general public.

Terminals In the Home

With such chaotic developments in the television industry, many of us tend to overlook the obvious—the fact that most people have at least three under-used and underrated terminals right in their homes:

1. the telephone
2. the radio, and
3. the television.

If these potential terminals do in fact eventually provide the basis for a communications "network" that is already a widespread part of American life, their statistics are startling. In 1978, 95 percent of American homes had telephones in them, as opposed to roughly one in three in the thirties. Radios are even more abundant: over 400 million of them in 1978.

Televisions, the most conspicuous candidates for video communications, are so plentiful that most Americans would find it difficult to live without them. Again in the same year, 16 there was a TV for every 1.8 persons in the United States.

Table 1–1.   A list of applications of teletext systems according to subject category.

General Info Services	Classified Ads	Professional Info Services	Business Applications	Message Communications	Shopping Aids	Education	Calculator Service	Reservations
News	Properties	Financial data	In-house info services	Electronic telegram	Market prices	Courses at home	Slide rule service	Hotels
Sports	Employment	Literature retrieval	In-house phone directories	Telex connection	Special offers	School homework service	Business calculations	Cars
Financial	Services	Technical info	Business info	Newspaper reporting	Mail order	Special coaching	Technical calculations	Travel
Entertainment	Articles for sale		Secretarial services	Phone for deaf		Adult education		Vacations
Time tables			Circulars					
Phone directories			Accounts info					
Yellow pages			Personnel					
Leisure								
Recipes								

Despite the verbal beating for the sit-coms' silliness and the programming profligacy, the tube is a part of our lives. Again, look at the statistics: the TV set is turned on for an average of 6.5 hours a day, and a typical viewer actually watches it 28 hours a week. Our lives have to be affected by such an ever present, imposing medium—sometimes for the better, sometimes for the worse. In the space of one half-hour, series actors can laugh themselves into and out of decisions on romance, divorce, surgery, jobs, pain, and separation. On the "dramatic" level, they weave their spine-tingling ways through beatings, shootings, auto crashes, plunges from windows, and an occasional shoe from the TV viewer. After the concluding commercials, no mention is ever made of the long-term lingering effects of such acts of violence, separation, or involvement. No care is taken to warn the viewer that TV-watching may be harmful to their emotional and intellectual health. No one can seriously argue with the proposition that, "No other contemporary product, other than the automobile and telephone, has been a more potent force in both shaping and accommodating modern lifestyles as the TV set. For millions of Americans, television absorbs more time than anything except sleep and work." This statement is taken from the International Resource Development report on "The Home Terminal," published in 1978.

If its past has been influential, the future of TV promises to be downright adventurous. The century to date has been but an extended overture to the last two decades. Bell, Marconi, Zworykin, and Sarnoff—among many others—have all initiated technological trends that will eventually focus on personalized video computer communications. Public television, pay TV, participatory programming, computer-assisted video instruction, media rooms, personal video communications, data base acquisition, and games are just some of the many, many existing possibilities. The prospects are so exciting that anyone who owns a computer and/or video equipment—or anyone who is thinking of a purchase—should seek to combine these maturing and new technologies into a highly convenient, instantaneous, and inexpensive means of communication. You can be a pioneer of the next phase in human communications.

After running through the various developments and applications in video technology, Ken Winslow, director of Public Television Library in Washington, D.C., says:

For the first time, full control of your use of television has passed into your own hands. Many new developments are in store for you. Welcome to the new era of home video communications.

Communicating Words And Pictures— Yesterday and Today

The world of communications is undergoing a radical mutation in every corner and at every crossroad of today's society. In the process, the long accepted historical distinctions among the media are blurring, fading away, and allowing the concepts of one to flow into the other. In recognition of this phenomenon, Federal Communications Chairman Charles Ferris stated in 1980: "Events are quickly making these classifications unwieldy if not sometimes incoherent. Traditional concepts are being blitzed by a revolution in the technology by which we communicate."

The traditional paper-and-manual-delivery methods of communication have had their day. The pace of our modern industrial societies has assumed such a high tempo that we cannot afford to "miss a beat." For the lack of crisply clear, comprehensive, lightning-quick communications, a manufacturing firm misses a large order, an ambulance arrives too late, or a missile is mistakenly launched. The need—our need to step up the sophistication of our communication capability—is great and becoming greater every day.

Yet, true to our dogged human nature, many of us cannot shake ourselves free of archaic, outmoded communication vehicles. We are content with our books, newspapers, magazines, letters, memos, and other "paper" media. In fact, we marvel at the speed at which developments on the other side of this globe are played out and analyzed on the evening news. Yet for most of our day-to-day activities, we still rely on the fast-fading paper media. As much as we look forward to spending a cold, rainy evening curled up in an overstuffed sofa with a good book, the printed media are destined to give way sooner or later. They must stand aside for the type of ordinary telecommunicating described at the start of this chapter. For once the general

19

public equips themselves through consumer purchases with the necessary hardware, electronic telecommunication can become an everyday thing—much as broadcast television and tele-phoning did in their days.

For the sake of historical contrast, let's consider how a book—this book—is produced. Book production requires a num-ber of time-consuming and expensive steps. First, the author writes the words either by hand or on a typewriter. If hand-written, the original draft must be typed by someone else for submission to the publisher. Anything that cannot be easily explained by words alone requires rough sketches by the author. These words and pictures are then submitted to the publisher. If acceptable, the words are keyed all over again at the typesetter's shop, and the art is drawn by a commercial artist or draftperson. Every time another keying or drawing takes place, the resultant output must be proofread, usually several times. The final version of the book, the reproduction copy, is then sent to a printer, who makes negatives, then plates, then printed sheets. The printed sheets are collated, folded, trimmed, and bound into books—which then must be either physically shipped to places where they may be sold or mailed out to buyers. Generally, this process takes months, sometimes years, because it is almost completely manual.

Yet we have become so used to communicating by means of printed material—books, newspapers, magazines, letters, memos—that we find it hard to imagine other ways.

Every book that deals with developments in either com-puter or video technology renders the book publishing industry that sponsored it a little quainter—pushes it a little closer to obsolescence. Facing more and more of a challenge to keep up with other media in communicating the latest information in all fields of human achievement, books come up against their most difficult task when they must convey the latest developments in computers or video equipment. As a result, book publishers have to generate their product faster and update it more often—despite rising material and labor costs. Ironically, in their effort to perpetuate the industry, they are gestating their progeny industry—computerized video communication.

Compared to the nearly instantaneous transmission and ongoing updating of video images or of data displays, books assume an archaic air, rather like a nineteenth-century stereopticon or the eighteenth-century clerk's quill pen.

In addition, consider the high-prices of distributing these books via the United States Postal Service, which is rapidly becoming an expensive nonservice, and you easily see why "there must be a better way."

The Communications "Lag"

Though particularly conspicuous in the case of books, the time-wasting production and distribution requirements of traditional media has led to a "communications lag." By the time a report, periodical, or book is actually published and distributed, the contents have aged, if not died—a stillborn child. This communications lag affects just about every part of our lives—education, business, science, government, and home life. In a fast-moving field, the information contained in books can be outdated before the ink is dry.

In education, this lag deprives the student of a better education. A school system is likely to "hang on" to a supply of textbooks, simply because they are relatively new and cannot be discarded before their standard "usage" time is up. Yet a video computer program can be updated periodically at little or no cost, depending on the system. Further, a textbook cannot carry a student's interest in the same way a video display can. Pupils take to computer-assisted instruction eagerly, clamoring for the chance to "play" with the device.

Business suffers from the communications lag also. Reports have to be compiled, organized, typed or typeset, and photocopied or printed before submission, sometimes via the mail or other physical delivery agent. By the time a manager actually reads and acts upon the information in a report, the information is old. This lag not only leaves the door open to serious errors in decision making, but it also makes upper management look as though they don't know what is "really" going on. As a result, supervisors and workers lose confidence in their management—perhaps even regarding them as "out of touch." If anything, photocopiers and fax transmitter devices have served only to increase the density of the so-called "paper blizzard," 21 making management's visibility factor even lower. A video computer network, however, offers fast, up-to-the-minute information at the push of a few buttons.

As just one example, George A. Champine (Univac's R&D Director) explained that the publisher of a recent book of his saved "months of production time" by automating the production procedure. Champine used one of his own development programs—a computer-based, remote text editing/typesetting system—to produce the book. Although he wrote the manuscript in longhand, one of his clerical staffers used the on-line system for typesetting and editing changes. Thus he saved the publisher thousands of dollars in keying and setting time, as well as getting the book to market sooner. He went on to state: "Executives cost a company about $60,000 per year apiece. A $2,000 terminal spread over a few years is a small price if it helps improve [their] efficiency." With automation, they can eliminate the "information float" that hurts the performance of companies keeping valuable information in transit when it could be in users' hands." In regard to independent terminals for use in distributed data processing systems and automated networks, he says, "They're coming like a tidal wave."

The world of science has demonstrated that, with better communication networks, the world-wide community of researchers work more efficiently and avoid failure/success duplication. For example, around the turn of the nineteenth century, two groups of engineers tried to build separate canals with locks of wood—each group ignorant of the other's efforts. They worked within twenty years and within three hundred miles of each other. Yet both met with the same failure, and both drew the same conclusion: You cannot build locks of wood.

Of course, with improved communication, such duplication of effort happens less today. Scientists—including medicos—still rely heavily on printed media to interchange their information and findings. Still, scientific printed material has become so abundant in recent years that no one person can read it all. Instead, specialists resort to reading only about their specialities and generalists must rely on synopses and abstracts to keep up-to-date. The recent appearance of computer data bases promises an easier way in the future, but such data distribution networks must be considered fetal in comparison to their full, long-range potential.

In government—and more specifically in defense—the country with the most sophisticated overall communications systems will prove to be the one with the quickest wartime reflex. Briefly, effective communications could mean national survival.

Delays, Delays

With all these goings-on in the video, computer, and office machine industries, our original scenario seems close at hand. The technology is here or at least fast approaching. People in all sectors of society want the changes to take place. What's the holdup?

A number of factors are delaying the advent of total electronic communications. Basically, they boil down to:

- Confusion about whether the communications media should be phone lines, coax cables, fiber optics, satellites, or some combination of these.
- Legal questions about the phone companies' right to restrict the use of their media and about the duties tied in with their franchises.
- A lack of compatibility among the pieces of hardware. Manufacturers put out equipment with different sets of specifications, few of which are compatible.
- Prices that still have to reach consumer-acceptance level.

THE MEDIUM

A search is going on for a standardized, efficient, and universal communications network. Amid the tangle of phone wires, coax cables, and fiber-optic lines, communications experts thrash out priorities and specifications: Can the existing phone line system handle standard video transmissions on a mass basis? Should it have to? Do we, in effect, have to "re-wire" the world with a type of cable that can handle the signals of the near future? Or are microwave transmissions via satellites the more feasible alternative? Which sort of cable and/or broadcast system will meet both present and future needs? What *are* those needs?

The essential question is, What's the most efficient way for one terminal to communicate with another? If the medium selected is truly the most efficient, within practical ranges, it should last us a good time. Going to the next-most-complicated question—although still a simplistic one—is communication by wire or by wire-less the better route?

Technical Difficulties Beyond Our Control. The term *wires*, of course, means phone lines or TV cables. Without going into great detail, suffice it to say that phone lines can transmit video data of only a limited nature. Also, they extend like a web all over the world; and wherever the lines do not go, satellites extend their reach almost everywhere. However, a video "picture" (of the type we are used to seeing broadcast by the networks) simply does not "fit" through a phone line; it requires too much electronic data in too fast a flow for the lines to carry it. TV cables, specially constructed and installed, *can* carry "regular" TV pictures, but they are not as omnipresent as phone lines nor are they as accessible.

Holding up the widespread use of phone lines for video transmissions, however, is the expense of purchase and installation. Right now the equipment costs too much and yields too little. Of all the subjects we deal with in this book, video transmission on a private basis—either through the air or over the phone lines—is about the least developed area. Perhaps, like a lurking giant, it is awaiting the other technological bits and pieces to fall together. Or maybe it is awaiting mass acceptance and the resultant drop in prices in the marketplace. In any case, the wave will break sooner or later; and when it does, television will belong to the private citizen—not to the network moguls.

Right now, not many companies are vying for the trade. Nippon Electric has licked the color problem in slow-scan TV and markets the DFP-751, but the cost is high. RCA had to abandon its Videovoice system for a combination of marketing and technical reasons, leaving the domestic market to the Bell System, Robot Research, and a few others.

Bell's product, the Picturephone, is a relatively inexpensive video camera and audio unit in a console. Its picture consists of 251 lines at 30 frames per second—pretty close to commercial TV. Yet one problem that limits the quality of the picture is the narrow bandwidth necessitated by the phone lines; normally audio phone lines have bandwidths of 3 kHz, whereas a good picture requires a width closer to 4 mHz.

Robot Research also puts out phone-line video transmission products, Models 510, 520, and 530. Each of these models utilizes a 128-line picture that takes 8.5 seconds of transmission time when converted to (audio) phone line bandwidths. Robot Research literature explains that though a full 525-line picture is possible on phone-line television (PLTV), it would require a three-minute transmission time. Since Robot's declared primary application is in security operations, the company's management has opted for a lower-quality picture that is transmitted faster.

Perhaps if some time in the future the Computer and Business Equipment Manufacturers Association (CBEMA) have their way with the FCC, the Commission will ban all restrictions on the use of phone lines, the market will thus become wide open, and more manufacturers will be tempted to compete for the consumer end of the business.

"Wire-less" approaches—broadcasting over the air waves—bypass the problem of "fitting" the signal into a line, but they raise other problems. Broadcasting requires stations with transmitting power and satellites for relay capability. The quality of broadcast signals, even those transmitted 70,000 kilometers by satellite relay, is fine. Also, while more satellites go up every year, the cost of using them is coming down. The prospects of broadcasting sound inviting, but how do you go about broadcasting your own signal?

That question sets off the economic from the technical aspects of the problem. While standardization might be considered a "technical" problem, its genesis and enhancement arise from economic motivation and from market manipulation. However, establishing a communications network is more clearly a technical, as opposed to an economic, problem. (Admittedly, it has legal implications, which we shall get to shortly.) Surprisingly, at least some of the technical kinks are being worked out by an unlikely group—the HAM radio operators of America. These amateurs of the air waves are rapidly breaking into TV, using a few extra dollars and usually second-hand equipment from here and there to develop personal TV broadcasting stations. We will evaluate their role late in the video chapter. 25

Suffice it to say now, however, that their work today could well qualify them for a place as the pioneers of personalized video communications.

The Long Reach
Of the Law

The legal restrictions affect not so much the equipment itself as they do the communications network. The "wires" of this country are presently controlled by AT&T or by various telephone companies, a half-dozen new carriers, or cable TV companies. Understandably, none of the owners is willing to permit the use of its lines without due compensation. Furthermore, phone companies are forbidden by the FCC to intermingle their facilities with cable TV, radio, or regular TV networks. They may sell the service on such lines, but not physically connect them to any other. Given these and the technical problems with video transmission over phone lines, the use of this medium is likely to take longer to work out than "wire-less" media.

So is the answer to take to the air? Use of the "air" for transmission purposes is controlled by the government, specifically by the Federal Communications Commission (FCC). As much as many Americans balk at the idea of the government's control of the "air," regulation in this area is essential. Presently, the broadcasting spectrum is packed with transmissions—network TV, radio programming, police and military communications, citizen band transmissions, HAM radio and TV, airline control communications and radar, shipping transmissions, among many others. In certain areas of the country where the population is dense, the mega-urban or megalopolis areas, the air is literally filled with transmissions of all kinds.

The problem is that, like so many other things today, transmission frequencies are limited. The transmission *band*, the total spectrum of wave frequencies, permits only so many users at a time. Putting an even greater burden on the band was the opening up of a part of this band to the "citizen." This "citizen band" (CB) usage soared to a peak in 1976, a year in which 10.5 million CB radios were sold. The overall effect of the CB phenomenon, which we will touch on later in the book, is that the already crowded air waves became saturated in certain densely populated areas.

The "crowded-air" is one of the problems facing not only the FCC, but also the developers of an IVT system. On a day-to-day basis, the FCC must take measures to ensure that one transmission does not interfere with others and that the priority communications take precedence. For instance, radiotelephone owners and HAM operators must obtain licenses before they may transmit. CBers must also obtain licenses, although the process is easier than obtaining a dog license; no tests or significant qualifications are necessary. Manufacturers, too, have to figure out new ways of utilizing the slice of the transmission spectrum that already belongs to them—such as in the development of the single-sideband CB transceiver for avoiding excessive crowding. Certain TV broadcasters now slip in data transmissions between the regular scanning intervals during programming; the viewers can either watch the regular programs (unaware of the data content of the broadcast) or "dial in" the data with a special, usually hand-held data terminal.

Obviously a great deal of compromising legislation and deregulation—or at least a reevaluation of the use of the airwaves—will be on the agenda before crowded private video transmission takes its place on the spectrum, alongside "All in the Family" and "10-4 Good Buddy!"

Fitting
The Pieces Together

Over the past few years retail stores have sold strange new electronic entertainment, energy control, computer, and other devices—with little or no regard for one product's compatibility with another. The public, still learning the uses and languages of these new devices, has to make more or less permanent purchase decisions when buying some of these new types of equipment.

Questions concerning various new capabilities confuse and sometimes prevent consumers from plunking down several hundreds of hard-earned dollars on a new device—whether they are buying computers or video equipment. Which programming language to use? Is a built-in computer monitor better than the home TV set? Will the computer work with any TV? Will other manufacturers' peripherals "fit" into a system built around a given microcomputer? Video equipment presents 27 even worse problems. Which kind of gadget-equipped TV is best? Will discs become user-recordable and user-programmable soon?

Unhappily, this indecision only compounds the standardization problem. Hardware continues to sweep over the nontechnical consumer, and manufacturers continue to produce it copiously to take advantage of the blossoming market. Little attention is paid to whether all the pieces fit together. Of the many personal computers on the market today, only small numbers of them can communicate with each other. Besides the fairly commonly accepted S-100 or S-800 bus and the IEEE 488 bus system, many computers require special communication and interface alterations (add-in boards). And aside from the basic 1800-rpm rotation speed for early video discs, little has been standardized in the video field.

The Declining
Price of Progress

While you can argue that a lack of compatibility gives the "idea" people free rein to create in any direction, it does put a kink in the integration process and keeps prices up. Once you have fairly universal compatibility in the hardware, you can look forward to mass production, which, if nothing else, drives prices *down*. As welcome as this situation is under any circumstances, it nonetheless presents the prospect with an unusual type of decision. The consumer has to decide whether to buy now, possibly at a higher price for an experimental product, or wait for next year and possibly for a cheaper, state-of-the-art product? For example, a Cincinnati student declared: "I love the new videotape recorders—but they are too expensive. Everyone I know plans to wait until the price comes down."

At the beginning of the eighties, the cost of these new gadgets, though dropping every year, is often just a trifle more than the average consumer is willing to pay. For example, assuming that a thousand dollars is the cut-off point for consumer markets (however arbitrary that figure may be), then much of the equipment necessary to create an isolated IVT falls above that level. Certainly the cost of the total IVT system, bought from scratch, is several times that figure. The marketing experts for electronics manufacturers, in the meantime, have to balance the market's eagerness to buy against product cost. At the thousand-dollar mark, this equation seems to balance out to zero, except for stereo and *HAM* radio buffs who quickly spend well over $1,000.

But the prices of all electronic equipment indicate that the equation will swing over in the early eighties in favor of the purchase. Most video and computer product lines presently straddle the cut-off point. For instance, video recorder/players are well below the thousand-dollar level, though their sales are constrained somewhat by the imminent development of the user-programmable disc player. Disk players promise at the very least to provide simplicity, to record more video, to be more compatible with quality projection and computer display screens, and generally to offer more search-and-branch features. But they also cost more for most of these features when they first came out. RCA's SelectaVision was the initial low-cost exception.

Black-and-white as well as color cameras are also coming down in price, making the television a convenient showcase for home "tapies." Porta-paks—consisting of a lightweight camera, small monitor for playback, and power supply—no longer hover over the consumer spending limit. Home computers range from as little as a few hundred dollars for the stripped-down models, through $1,500–$2,000 for "loaded" home systems, to several thousands for the tabletop turnkey full business systems.

Yet every indication is that the prices of equipment are going down and going down fast. Much of this is due to pressure from Japanese and European TV manufacturers. Each year brings models that cost less and that offer more desirable integrated features. As the products become more mass-advertised and pragmatically attractive—and the prices lower—more and more prospects will buy for energy conservation, entertainment, education, safety, and other applications. At a certain point in such a market situation, the cause becomes the effect, and the effect becomes the cause. In other words, the eagerness to buy is the cause of greater production volumes and consequently lower unit prices. If the buying demand is great enough, production will increase and prices will drop to the point at   *29* which they become the cause of even greater buying eagerness. Thus the effect becomes the cause and the cause, the effect.

The Integrated Video Terminal (IVT)

At the eye of these whirlwind developments lies the need for a new and unifying concept of communications. The traditional concepts simply do not measure up to our needs today. And while manufacturers try in various ways to fill those needs, they fashion their products after corporate goals and policies, not after a universal concept. Considered objectively at a distance, their collective efforts seem somewhat aimless. They have all the capability, but they do not have the concept that would put that capability to work most effectively and suitably. They lack the concept that would bring all this power to a focus.

The communications concept needed today must, within practical limitations, offer:

- instantaneous transmission,
- universal compatibility,
- up-to-the-minute accuracy, and
- comprehensive information.

Hence the integrated video terminal, or video computer as it is sometimes called.

THE UNADORNED SYSTEM

For the moment, forget the technicalities that cloud the essentially simple concept. Ignore, temporarily, the difficulties with deregulation, cost, media, compatibility. Strip away all the objections, and you see that the concept is actually quite simple.

The integrated video terminal is a combination of video equipment (a screen and recorder/player) and computer hardware (processor, I/O devices, and external storage). See Figure 1–2. Ideally, the IVT's components should all be capable of working together. For instance, the system should have one screen for both digital data and video displays. And the recording medium for the video components should double as external storage for the computer elements.

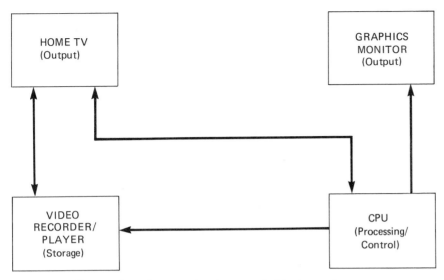

figure 1–2   The simplistic diagram of an integrated video/computer.

Aside from the basic components shown in Figure 1–2, the IVT system can grow as needed through the addition of other accessories, perhaps the most important of which is the communications adaptors. With this, the video/data report becomes just about instantaneous, despite the geographic dispersion of the users. Meetings can be called in seconds, adjourned in minutes—with the proper terminals and communication network. For widespread application in homes, businesses, schools, hospitals, government, and elsewhere, the IVT must be able to communicate with other similar systems freely, as people now do verbally by phone. The displays should be storable either as pictures in the video components or as data in the computer memory. Both types of displays should be mixable for either display, modification, or communications.

The IVT is *not* many things. It is not just a video recorder/player with a video-chip built in for bells and whistles. It is not just a TV screen that responds to voice commands. And it is not just a home computer that draws pictures on a TV screen. Although all these developments reflect the "tinkering" instinct in R&D people, and although they all point toward overall integration sometime in the future, they are only milestones on the road toward some sort of IVT configuration. Admittedly, such a configuration could not stand still—not arrive at some "perfect" status beyond which no further development is needed.

The IVT concept is a type of technological watershed. Many minor and seemingly unrelated developments trickle like tributaries toward a pooling of thought. Compelled by the natural energy of gravity, the waters have no choice but to converge and commingle. At the watershed, a synergistic effect takes hold. It's happened before with many other electronic devices and with the application of electricity itself. For decades, theoretical scientists tinkered with the effects of electricity. Then came one watershed after another: the telegraph, telephone, radio, television, and so on. We don't think of these common communication devices as "watersheds," but they are.

The IVT can be many times more pervasive in its effect on our lives because the streams that feed the concept derive from other watersheds that were all-pervasive in their day. At the same time, the low-grade electronic breakthroughs that are becoming commonplace are also feeding the technological pool. It's really just a matter of time.

THE FEEDER STREAMS

Developments in all areas—video equipment and communications, data processing and communications hardware, telecopying devices, telephone and satellite networks, and many others—are trickling toward a sudden pooling.

Video Displays. The mainstreams of video and computer developments, although separate, are quickly converging. How are the two streams "separate"? Essentially, the differences lie in the nature of the two types of display. In an IVT, the video display must encompass basically two areas:

1. *The video form* we refer to arbitrarily as a display of any kind of visual image that may be recorded from a television screen or video camera; it does not consist of data. Rather it consists of pure image in the form in which the human eye views a subject in the "analog" form. This type of display is secured from a camera or from a standard image on the TV set, whether that image comes via broadcasting, cable, or other means.

figure 1–3 *Video Display:* This television delivers not only the normal sort of video display that we are used to seeing on our sets, but it also delivers printed color pictures. The printed picture signal, which is "multiplexed" over the broadcast wave, triggers a printing mechanism in the set. Will advertisers be able to "send" you an order blank as you watch their commercials?

2. *The data form* is a display comprised of the normal input for the computer's central processing unit, that is, data entered by any kind of input device—keyboard, sensors, voice, and so on. Hence it is digital by nature. This sort of display, on the screen or on a printout, may take the form of statements in English, charts and graphs, or dynamic (often colorful) configurations.

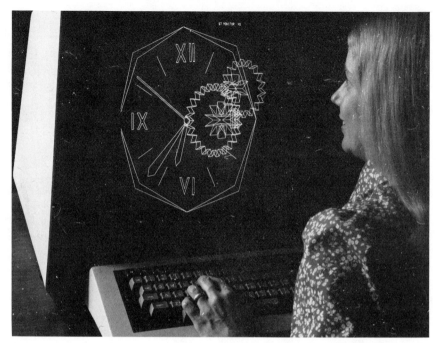

Courtesy: Sanders Associates, Inc.

figure 1–4 *Data Display:* This Graphic 7 intelligent display terminal is capable of a three-dimensional view of a rotating clock, with moving hands, gears, and pinions. The system can also stop the rotation, view the clock from any angle, reset time, or rotate at different speeds.

Whereas the source of video displays is purely visual, the generation of data displays relies on the accumulation and processing of data bits according to a given program. Obviously, the source of video displays is the video equipment, while the origin of data displays is in the computer. Although these definitions are painfully obvious, they are absolutely essential to an understanding of the IVT and its capabilities. The IVT concept is one in which Voltaire's admonition is especially important: "When you speak to me, define your terms."

The ideal video terminal combines video and data displays so as to present words and pictures in totally new, even revolutionary configurations. These configurations might be as simple as a menu of recipes for the chief cook in the household. Or they may be as complex as a three-dimensional data display, superimposed on a plant-growth video image, that tracks the maturation of the plant in tandem with several other curves for light exposure, nutrient absorption, and other environmental factors. (See Figure 1–2.)

The fundamental incompatibility between the two types of display is an essential characteristic of systems as they stand now. The video image is "recorded," whereas the other is "input." The data image is fairly easily transmitted over existing phone lines, but its video counterpart requires a much wider bandwidth than these lines can accommodate. Perhaps most important, their storage media differs essentially: "Video" images are analog, and "data" displays are digital. As a result, any integrated display of video and data entails a lot of chin-pawing and head-scratching over conversions between analog and digital signals. Hence the separation of these two mainstreams.

Their convergence seems to lie with breakthroughs in mass storage and in A/D/A conversion circuits, which, as we'll see, are encouragingly close at hand.

The IVT is the communication medium of the future, the vehicle for the interchange of meaningful words and pictures. In fact, one report predicted its appearance as a factory-made unit by 1982; this excellent report, put out by International Resource Development quoted a price in 1979 of $1,400!* The video computer is the culmination of most of the major developments in communications since the practical use of electricity. The phone, the TV, the radio, the computer, and the electronic camera are all manifestations of a technology searching for its ultimate form—a microminiaturized configuration that processes, stores, sends, receives, and reproduces.

THE CONFIGURATION

The simplistic diagram in Figure 1–1 is therefore only a starting point for the type of terminal that will come into wider and wider use as time goes by. Anyone with a grain of technical know-how can see, however, that Figure 1–1 does not tell the whole story. Given the economic, technical, and legal problems already discussed, the configuration can never be as simple as shown in this illustration. Constructing a video/computer terminal entails overcoming four basic problems:

*The IRD also publishes electronic mail and message systems. International Resource Development Inc., is a leading research firm in the office automation area.

Problem 1: To select an output device that is capable of diversified types of display, from simple character representations or taped showings to complex display and video combinations.

Problem 2: To select peripheral or interface devices that make the otherwise incompatible outputs of video and computer components suitable for display on the same screen and for storage in the same medium.

Problem 3: To select, when available, an external storage medium that is capable of handling the two kinds of display information and all supporting software. The storage medium should be compatible with video as well as with computer components in the system.

Problem 4: To select a communications medium that is economical, available to all users, and adequate for video transmission.

Problem 1: The CRT Display. The problems with display are tied up with the video recording and computer processing functions so inextricably that two chapters are needed to isolate and define the issues. Therefore Chapter 2 deals with graphic display from the video point of view, while Chapter 3 approaches the matter from the computerist's point of view.

Problem 2: Compatibility. Since the digital output of computer components will likely have to be stored in some way on a medium common to video equipment, then certain conversion devices are necessary to feed the data to the common graphics display device and to return it for storage on the common medium, as necessary. Chapter 4 examines the A/D/D/A problem, and what people are doing about it. Since it is so confusedly bound up in the secondary storage issue, it will necessarily overlap with that problem.

Problem 3: Secondary Storage. Video information is recorded, stored, and transmitted in analog form, while computer information is processed, stored, and communicated in digital form. The storage device for an integrated video/computer terminal therefore must store information in one form or another. Barring a technological breakthrough of great magnitude, the most common form until 1982 will probably still be analog. The

digital information of the computer thus becomes an interme-
diary form of data manipulation. The storage medium in the
near future is likely to be very different from present media,
possibly taking the form of magnetic bubble or laser/optical
videodisc.

Problem 4: Communications. Communications is one aspect
of the video/computer system that is the least controllable by
the individual user. Yet a mass trend toward standardization of
individual terminals will undoubtedly have a tremendous effect
on the medium finally selected for video transmission. If the
FCC, the television networks, and the electronics manufacturers
can identify a clearcut demand big enough to warrant their
attention, then a major (and probably hasty) reevaluation of the
traditional vehicles of communication and transmission will be
forthcoming. Chapter 5 therefore deals with problems that are
largely beyond the control of the individual user but that will be
on the horizon if enough enthusiasts make a spontaneous and
collective effort to create the demand.

From the overly simplified to the confusingly complex, we
try to disentangle the many cords that make up the knot. We
take each problem at a time, isolate it as much as possible,
and discuss how they're rapidly being solved.

chapter **2**

The Video Enthusiast's Point of View

When is a TV set not a TV set? In an integrated video/computer system, is the CRT screen video equipment or computer hardware? The answer is that it is both. The television set—the "video terminal" that has entertained us for years—suffices for game, home, and other personal computer applications. Yet when the applications become sophisticated, the "TV" becomes a "display screen," "a CRT," or "a monitor." This change in terminology reflects not only a shift in the user's regard for the device, but also a real difference in the makeup of the equipment.

Notice in Figure 2–1 (a duplicate of Figure 1–1) that the CPU feeds output to a "graphic output" device as well as to a home TV set. The reason for two screens is basically the incompatibility between the analog video image and the digital computer output. The analog–digital interfaces in the figure are not as easy as shown in the diagram—as we know—but they are *not* impossible. At the core of the problem is the hardware: A home TV accepts computer input only after a process called "modulation," whereas output from a video recorder cannot be displayed on a computer monitor without conversion to digital form. To understand when a TV stops becoming a "TV" and when it becomes an "output device," this chapter contains a review of the conventional video process and current video equipment.

figure 2–1   The simplified IVT system.

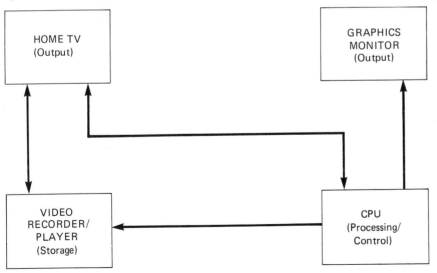

The Conventional
Video Process

In a sentence, the video process consists of three steps:

1. the conversion of light images into an electronic flow and eventually into a signal,
2. the transmission of the signal to a receiver set, and
3. the reconversion of the electronic signal into a visible light image.

The respective pieces of hardware for each of these steps are: (1) the camera, (2) the transmitter, and (3) the TV receiver set.

THE CAMERA

Black-and-White Cameras. Simplistically, the video camera converts the visual image into an electronic signal (Figure 2–2). As the light from the image strikes the accelerator grid, it is transformed into an electron flow, which is then passed on to the target plate. This electron flow creates an electronic charge

figure 2–2   A simple diagram of the video camera.

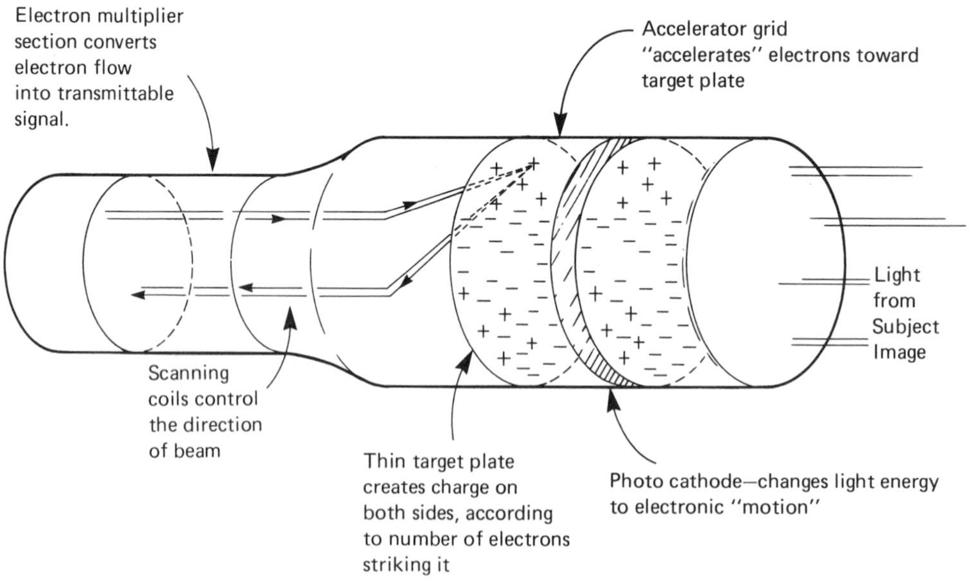

Electron multiplier section converts electron flow into transmittable signal.

Accelerator grid "accelerates" electrons toward target plate

Scanning coils control the direction of beam

Thin target plate creates charge on both sides, according to number of electrons striking it

Photo cathode—changes light energy to electronic "motion"

Light from Subject Image

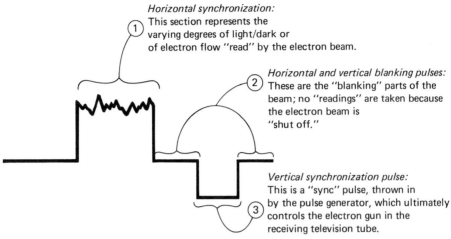

Horizontal synchronization:
① This section represents the varying degrees of light/dark or of electron flow "read" by the electron beam.

Horizontal and vertical blanking pulses:
② These are the "blanking" parts of the beam; no "readings" are taken because the electron beam is "shut off."

Vertical synchronization pulse:
This is a "sync" pulse, thrown in
③ by the pulse generator, which ultimately controls the electron gun in the receiving television tube.

figure 2–3   A diagram of either a vertical or horizontal black-and-white scanning wave.

distribution over both sides of the plate at once. The electron-scanning beam "reads" this charge in sequence. The beam strikes the plate and then bounces back to the degree that they encounter a charge in the plate. In other words, if the electron beam strikes a highly positively charged area, many of the electrons are absorbed and few are reflected. In relatively low-charged areas, more electrons are reflected. The return beam is therefore the basis for the transmittable electrical signal.

To manipulate the electron beam in a scanning motion across the target ring, the camera needs five kinds of pulses or signals (Figure 2–3):

1. The *horizontal synchronization* pulse starts and stops the horizontal trace.
2. The *horizontal blanking* pulse turns the electron beam *off* while the beam tracks back to the starting point.
3. The *vertical synchronization* (or *sync*) pulse starts and stops the vertical trace.
4. The *vertical blanking* signal does the same to the beam vertically as the horizontal blanking pulse does horizontally.
5. The *equalizer pulse*, not available in 1/2" or 1/4" tape equipment, starts the vertical scan every sixtieth of a second and keeps the horizontal oscillator "in sync" during the vertical retrace (Figure 2–4).

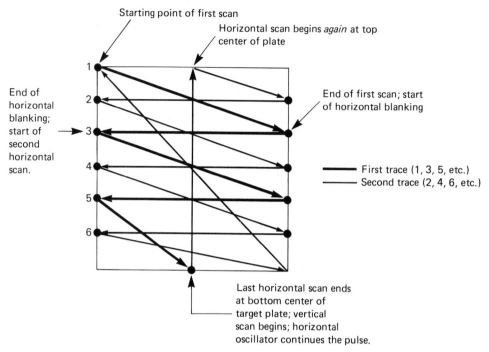

Starting point of first scan

Horizontal scan begins *again* at top center of plate

End of horizontal blanking; start of second horizontal scan.

End of first scan; start of horizontal blanking

—— First trace (1, 3, 5, etc.)
—— Second trace (2, 4, 6, etc.)

Last horizontal scan ends at bottom center of target plate; vertical scan begins; horizontal oscillator continues the pulse.

figure 2–4 The first series of horizontal scans reads every other line. After the vertical retrace, the second series reads the set of lines that the first series does not.

All these pulse, signals, frequencies—whatever you wish to call them—are generated by the pulse generator and influence the direction of the electron beam inside the camera. In black-and-white cameras the vertical frequency is 60 Hz (that is, it occurs every sixtieth of a second). The horizontal frequency is 15.75 kHz; it occurs 15,750 times a second. This frequency bears on the rest of the discussion.

Color Cameras. In color video cameras, the waveforms are more complicated. Three guns inside the camera pick up the initial voltages of the red, blue, and green (RGB) elements in the light striking the lens. The guns, equipped with light-sensors to enable them to differentiate color, produce three distinct signals:

1. The *luminance* ("light" or y) signal modulates the carrier frequency.
2. The *chrominance* ("color") signals modulate a second and third carrier, respectively.

Cameras may use one to four guns to carry this video information:

1. *Single-gun* cameras carry *all* the video information.
2. *Double-gun* cameras use one gun to carry the luminance (y) signal and the other to carry the RGB elements.
3. *Triple-gun* cameras use one gun for each color, and the y signal is then added to these signals before transmission.

Cameras produce various levels of quality in the picture at the receiving/recording end of a transmission network. Since the quality of a color picture depends more on the intensity of light than on the color itself, mixing the three colors for full-color pictures involves only three parameters:

1. hue (or tint),
2. saturation (or color), and
3. luminance (or intensity).

A fully saturated blue, for instance, is deep and rich. Add more light or luminance, and it turns progressively paler. Certain controls on the camera enable the user to employ the camera in various ways (Figure 2–5.)

figure 2–5   The basic camera.

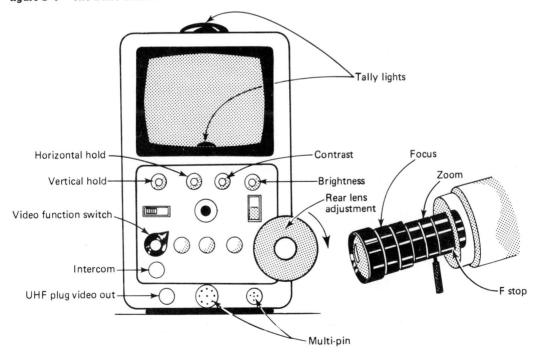

Table 2-1.   What to look for in color cameras

Color System:	Look for NTSC-type output, with a phase and frequency separation system
Vidicon Tube:	If single tube system, how does it compare with a multiple-gun system?
Scanning System:	525 lines, 60 Hz, 2:1 interlaced in the usual specification.
Video Output:	Check the number of pins per cable connector to see if it matches your video recorder plug; also 75 ohms is the standard impedance.
Resolution:	More than 230 lines (horizontal) and more than 300 lines (vertical) are standard.
S/N Ratio:	Compare the decibel ratings for the luminance and chroma channels: the higher the better.
Optimum Illumination:	This specification refers to the light (measured) in lux) in which the camera operates best. Look also for the **range** of light in which recording is possible. Compare with "Minimal practical illumination."
Automatic Light Compensation:	With this feature, the camera automatically adjusts video output level when light level (illumination) changes.
Microphone:	The mike should be built-in and omni-directional.
Audio Output:	Again, check the impedance and pins of the cable connectors for compatibility.
Lens Mounting System:	"C" mount is almost universal
Lens:	If the lens is a zoom, the iris should be automatic.
Viewfinder:	An electronic viewfinder is becoming more and more standard; it allows operator to see what the camera sees.
Operating Temperature Range:	Obviously, the wider the range, the better.
Accessories Provided:	A power supply, a daylight filter, a camera cable, and a battery case with handle are minimally acceptable.

"Chip" Cameras.   Although they cost no less than $1,000—and in some cases as much as $5,000—"chip" cameras are part of research and development budgets all over the world. These cameras employ charge-coupled devices (CCDs) that enable manufacturers to pack great resolution into extremely compact cameras. In 1979, Matsushita Electronics Corp., for example, 44 was developing a black-and-white CCD video camera with 512 pixels (picture elements) vertically by 486 horizontally. That 248,832-element grid provides a resolution, the firm maintains, of 360 by 350 lines. Nippon Electronics Corporation was also working on a chip camera with 285 by 480 lines, along with color filters for separation. At the same time the Germans were working on the FAC 1800, a compact, single-tube chip camera with an electronic viewfinder; and the Dutch firm, Philips readies its V200, a 3-vidicon-tube CCD camera for sale at prices under $1,500. In the States, RCA Electro-Optics planned a 3-CCD color camera that they hoped to price initially at $4,000 to $5,000 but that eventually would be available for mass production at far lower prices. The consumer-priced CCD video camera cannot be more than a couple of years away.

TRANSMISSION

Video. Camera signals are combined with the normal scanning signal, amplified for transmission, and then broadcast to receiving sets. When color signals are combined with the horizontal and vertical frequencies, the signals are slightly altered: The horizontal becomes 15.734 Hz, and the vertical 59.95 Hz. These changes preclude interference from harmonics among the various elements of the complicated signal.

figure 2–6   A diagram of the video broadcasting process.

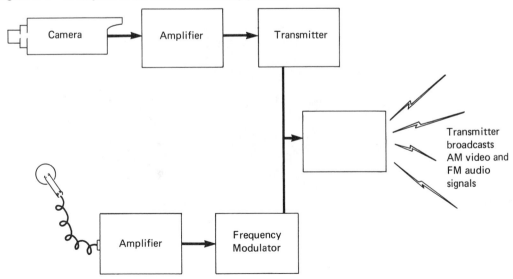

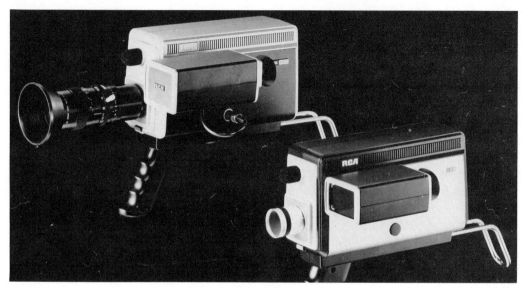

figure 2–7   CC001 has an adjustable shoulder rest, a 25-mm lens, and built-in microphone. The deluxe version, CC002, has a professional grade-6 power zoom lens with adjustable iris, which is found on many commercial cameras that sell for thousands of dollars. The CC002 has an electronic viewfinder that lets you frame the picture, focus, or zoom in without taking your eye off the viewfinder. A miniature black-and-white TV monitor with a 1.5" screen lets you see what the camera sees.

figure 2–8   This $1,095 portable videocassette system includes Akai's VC-300 black-and-white camera and the VT-300 videocassette recorder, which features a small instant-feedback screen (lower left). The recorder uses 1/2" 30-minute cassettes. The camera has a 16-mm lens and built-in microphone.

Courtesy: Hitachi

figure 2–9   The Hitachi video color camera, which retails for $1,200 in Japan, is shown here with its optional viewfinder and zoom lens; the microphone is built-in. Using a single tube, it makes automatic color hue and saturation adjustments while zooming.

figure 2–10   The Toshiba IK-12 features an instant playback mini-monitor on the side of the camera and a separate power supply unit. It utilizes a single-gun system.

Courtesy:
Toshiba America, Inc.

figure 2–11 This Japan Victor Corporation (JVC) portapak enables the user to take color "tapies" anywhere. From left to right are the AC power adaptor, the cassette recorder, the color compensator, and the two-gun color camera.

figure 2–12 The Panasonic VHS camera requires only normal room lighting and uses a single vidicon tube. The WV-2900 weighs in at only 5 pounds and measures 4″ × 11 7/16″ × 2″. The standard C-mount lens accepts other C-mount lenses easily. Optional accessories include a 1 1/2″ electronic viewfinder with light intensity indicator.

figure 2–13 The VZ-CT20 is a color camera so small that it fits easily into one hand, and it is so sensitive that you can take pictures at night with ordinary home lighting. Its high sensitivity is due to an improved "Newvicon" tube that is more than three times as sensitive as those used in other cameras.

figure 2–14 Panasonic's hand-held VHS color cameras—(a) PK 200 and (b) PK-300—offer excellent color reproduction at normal room light conditions. With C-mount lenses and a built-in condenser microphone, they include remote trigger controls, tripod mounting holes, electromagnetic focusing, color temperature switches, and internal synchronization.

Courtesy: Sony **figure 2–15** Sony, the company that started all the excitement about home video, has a portable color camera and portable Betamax player/recorder, on the market. The Betamax, with a battery pack, can also be used in the home, connecting to any standard TV set.

Audio. If audio is also involved, the microphone sends the audio signal first to an amplifier and then to a frequency modulator, which integrates the sound waves with the video signals and carrier waves. The composite signal is then transmitted (Figure 2–6).

Transmission may take place in one of two forms:

1. broadcasting over the air waves, or
2. cablecasting through a line.

THE BROADCASTING "SQUEEZE"

When the composite signal is sent out by the transmitting station, the wave must fit into a band in the overall wave spectrum. Thus broadcasting becomes part of the "crowded-air" syndrome facing the FCC today, a problem that ultimately bears on the communications capability of the video/computer terminal. Putting TV transmission into the proper perspective at this point seems appropriate.

All waves—including those from distant stars signaling the death of a great sun or those from the local TV station advertising the newest underarm deodorant—are part of an overall radio wave spectrum (Table 2–2). The waves in this spectrum vary in length from the extremely long to the extremely short, and a wave's position on the spectrum depends on its wavelength.

Table 2–2. The Radio Spectrum

Classification (Abbrev.)	Frequency		Wavelengths (m & cm)
	kHz/sec.	mHz/sec.	
Very low frequency (VLF)	Less than 30	—	Over 10,000 m
Low frequency (LF)	30-300	—	10,000–1,000 m
Medium frequency (MF)	300-3,000	.3-3.0	1,000–100 m
High frequency (HF)	—	3-30	100–10 m
Very high frequency (VHF)	—	300-3,000	1m (100 cm)–10 cm
Ultra high frequency (UHF)	—	3,000-30,000	10–1cm
Extremely high frequency (EHF)	—	30,000-300,000	1–0.1 cm

A television transmitter creates a radio wave much like radio. The power source in the transmitter sends a current up and down an antenna, reversing the direction of the flow in such a way as to create a pulsating magnetic field around the antenna. With each pulsation, an "electromagnetic" wave is sent off from the antenna. As the current changes direction more quickly, the waves are generated more frequently, and they are sent out closer together. In other words, the faster pulses generate the higher frequencies. These radio frequencies are called "RFs." As the distance from the crest of one wave to the crest of another becomes greater, the wavelength becomes longer. In Figure 2–16, the relationship between wavelength and frequencies is demonstrated pictorially. The wavelengths

figure 2–16   The broadcasting system.

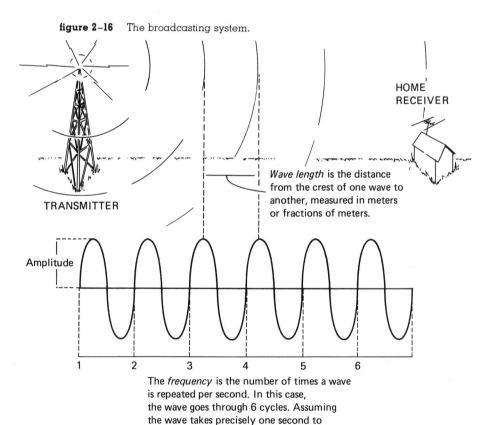

HOME
RECEIVER

Wave length is the distance from the crest of one wave to another, measured in meters or fractions of meters.

TRANSMITTER

Amplitude

1   2   3   4   5   6

The *frequency* is the number of times a wave is repeated per second. In this case, the wave goes through 6 cycles. Assuming the wave takes precisely one second to travel from the transmitter to the receiver, then it is a 6-cycle frequency—or 6 hertz; 60,000 times a second would be 60 megahertz. (mHz) and frequencies are far out of proportion, because no artist could draw the necessary thousands of cycles on a page this size and still show what we want to show. In fact, if the drawing were an exact representation, the transmitter and receiver would defy Newtonian physics by being in the same place at the same time!

Assuming the diagram is feasible—for the sake of a point—what kind of radio frequency is emanating from one point to another? Commercial television stations broadcast in either the very high frequencies (VHF) or ultra high frequencies (UHF). Table 2–2 shows that these bands include the 300 to 3,000 megahertz and the 3,000 to 30,000 megahertz bands, respectively.

What Is a Megahertz?   The word "hertz" means "cycle." (Other technical distinctions make a hertz different from a cycle, but for the sake of our explanation, you can assume that the two are one in the same.) In Table 2–2, you see the whole radiowave spectrum laid out in terms of its relative blocks of frequencies and wavelengths. Because the spectrum is so vast, it cannot be easily measured in cycles, or hertz, alone. So scientists and engineers have grouped thousands of hertz into kilohertz (kHz) and millions of hertz into megahertz (mHz). Grouping them this way simply eliminates the use of a lot of numbers. In other words, 300,000,000 hertz is equal to 300,000 kilohertz and to 300 megahertz. Obviously, 30,000,000,000,000 wave cycles occurring in a time frame of one second may truly be called "ultrahigh frequency."

These high frequencies are necessary because commercially broadcast images require the fast transmission of a great deal of electronic information. Hence the frequencies must be very or ultra high.

Actually the video information is carried "in the middle" of RF wave (Figure 2–17). The wave that goes out from a transmitter is actually threefold: (1) a carrier frequency, (2) the signal frequency plus the carrier, and (3) the carrier frequency minus the signal frequency. For example, assume the signal (video/audio information wave) is 1,000 Hz (or 1,000 cycles per second). Further assume that the carrier frequency is 1,000,000 Hz. The three-part signal would consist of a carrier (100,000 Hz) in   *53* between two signals of 1,000 Hz each. The carrier is the *band-width*, and the two signals constitute the *sidebands*. One sideband is only a mirror image of the other. A TV channel has a bandwidth of 6 mHz, and the lower sideband is suppressed. When one sideband is blocked out, the transmission is considered to be *single-sideband*.

Although waves can be modulated either in frequency (FM) or amplitude (AM), TV broadcasts are amplitude modulated. The amplitude is the "height" of the wave (see Figure 2–16). The amplitude depends on the amount of power causing the wave. When the video signal is modulated for TV transmission, the transmitter's power is divided among the three parts of the wave: 50 percent to the carrier and 25 percent to each signal. The resulting signal is diagrammed as shown in Figure 2–17.

figure 2–17   The RF waveform: The modulating frequency's amplitude represents the power of the transmitter.

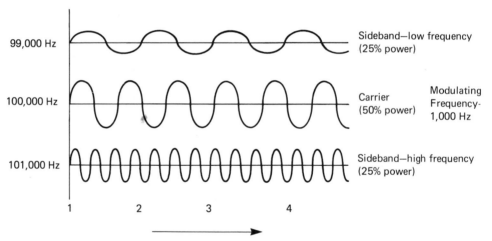

99,000 Hz — Sideband—low frequency (25% power)

100,000 Hz — Carrier (50% power) / Modulating Frequency-1,000 Hz

101,000 Hz — Sideband—high frequency (25% power)

1   2   3   4

Two factors influence the effectiveness of transmission: the power of the transmitter and the antenna. The distance that a signal can be sent depends greatly on the power source sending the current up and down the antenna: the higher the power source, the farther the wave travels. Most TV transmitting antennas are omnidirectional, which broadcasts a signal in all directions at once. Physical obstructions and electrical interference cut down on the distance a signal travels. For instance, if an antenna is located on an isolated hilltop in a rural area, the signal travels farther than if the antenna were situated in a heavily built-up area with a lot of electrical interference.

Ham TV. The HAM operator has long been the unsung hero of the air waves. What the CBer does within short ranges on the highways and byways, the HAM operator does on a wider— sometimes global—scale. HAM radio operators are the big-time amateurs. Operating on 9.5 to 9.725 mHz, which puts them into the high-frequency category according to Table 2–2, they can broadcast with a power source of up to 500 watts. Their range is potentially world-wide, with the right conditions.

HAM video and audio transmission has become especially attractive after 1975, when the FCC granted amateur operators permission to construct repeaters. Repeaters are stations that receive a signal, boost it a little, then restransmit it. The purpose, of course, is to make a signal go as far as it can go. The retransmitted wave is usually of a lower and stronger frequency.

Perhaps the biggest repeaters of all are OSCARs, satellites placed in space as Orbital Satellites Carrying Amateur Radio. The first OSCAR was launched in 1961. In March of 1978 OSCAR 8 want up to a 900-mile polar orbit, powered by solar cells. With this satellite, HAM operators can communicate at distances of up to 4,900 miles, but only when the satellite is in the right position. The repeater service is not a twenty-four-hour proposition. But Phase III of the satellite program should take care of that problem, providing around-the-clock repeater service. But that kind of service was not due until about late 1979. In the meantime, at least one computer/HAM enthusiast had designed a program to track the OSCAR and to compute the times it is avilable for HAMs. By early 1978, with the onset of the low-cost video camera, two-way HAM communication of television signals became feasible.

But a distinction must be made between the type of picture a HAM operator transmits and the kind you see on a commercial TV broadcast. Commercial TV, or animated TV, is usually referred to as "fast-scan." Insofar as a good, sharp picture usually requires about 525 lines per frame and about 30 frames per second, the electron beam "painting" the picture onto the CRT has to be extremely fast. Hence "fast" scan.

HAM TV, however, is called "slow-scan," because it consists of only 128 lines in 8 seconds. The picture, as a result, is a great deal coarser and is not animated as is your favorite commercial program (Figure 2–18). The basic reason is that while commercial television is broadcast on a bandwidth of 3.5

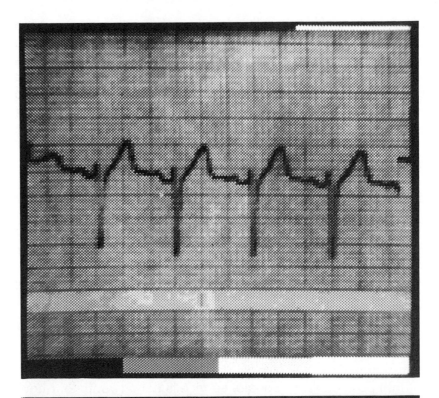

Courtesy:
Robot Research, Inc.

figure 2–18   These pictures are about the best that can be had right now on slow-scan TV (SSTV). They are supplied by the people who make the Robot Scan Converter which is the amateur's equipment for television broadcasting.

mHz, HAM operators are confined to only 1 kHz of bandwidth, which is really only enough for good voice transmission. So instead of continuous motion, the HAM receiver gets a series of "slides" at 8-second intervals.

It's a beginning!

Setting up a two-way video station can be as simple or as complicated, as expensive or as inexpensive, as you make it. You need certain types of equipment, a little ingenuity, and the desire to transmit and receive personalized pictures from all over the world. Here is a basic set-up:

1. A second-hand, black-and-white television set, preferably with a UHF tuner. If the set does not have one, you may have to purchase or rig up a converter to receive UHF frequencies. Since the picture is not going to be of commercial quality, don't worry about getting a brand-new sharply focused set.
2. A video camera of any variety, again second-hand if you can get one. Be careful especially of the lens sizes and mounts, because there are several different kinds: the 1" (25 mm) or 2/3" (16 mm) lens usually takes a C mount, whereas a 1/2" (8 mm) lens usually takes a D mount.
3. A transmitter in the 439.24 mHz neighborhood—it doesn't have to be right on the nose. A Motorola T-44 or an RCA CMU-15 are both fine.
4. A modulator that will convert the AM wave from the 1 volt coming from the camera to the 12, 25, or 70 volts you need for transmission.
5. An antenna made of low-cost coaxial cable, or "coax." Remember that you need a high "capture area" because UHF behaves oddly at times, sometimes here and sometimes there. A horizontal layout, rather than vertical, is better. Most important, the antenna must be above "ground level" whether that level is actually at the ground, at the tree tops, or at the ridgeline next to your house.

If you buy as much second-hand equipment as possible and price any new equipment carefully, taking advantage of discounts where possible, you can set up your own television station for as little as $135 to $500. A $1,000 would make a fine station indeed.

With such a station you can expect to broadcast for about 15 to 30 miles on the average. With top-notch equipment and good conditions, you could reach 60 to 100 miles.

While such developments may seem like nothing more than an interesting hobby—which they are—they will undoubtedly lead to communication links that were unthinkable a decade ago. For instance, in May of 1978 doctors in Florida and Hawaii held a panel discussion, viewed by some two hundred medical students at both locations, via television transmission by satellite. Although transmission was slow-scan, the potential is self-evident: Should a medical emergency arise in Florida, why not let a TV HAM get a slow-scan picture to Hawaii, if Hawaii had the only doctor who could make the correct diagnosis and prescribe the proper treatment?

With such diligent hobbyists at work, personalized video transmission over the air becomes feasible. The HAM radio network is at least an antecedent—and maybe a progenitor—of a universal personal video network.

Cable TV. Partially in reaction to the blandness of most broadcast programming and partially because broadcast signals simply do not reach certain areas, viewers are turning more and more to cable TV. Some systems use cable only to extend high-quality service to areas that, because of their geographic location, do not have good reception over the air. Other systems use cable exclusively in order to provide special programming, like Warner Communications in Ohio.

A total cable system consists of a series of increasingly smaller lines. The *trunk* line, the heaviest, is the main distribution cable. Its signal loss is generally low, but the loss increases as the line is tapped into for further branching to different areas. The lines branching off the trunk are called *feeders*, and they feed the signal to *drop* lines which carry the signal to the individual viewer's set. A transformer at the cable hookup to the VHF antenna terminal matches impedances.

At the other end of the cable system—the *headend* or point of origin—signals may be fed into the lines either from taped or live subjects. (Edited tapes at the headend sometimes cause trouble in cablecasting.) The signal is fed into an amplifier in which it is RF-modulated for a VHF station not in use in the area. When the signal from a tape (original or edited) is received at the home end, it may be fine for viewing on the TV set, but it may be difficult to tape on a video recorder because of differences in the timebases from the broadcast to 1/2" types.

If taping a cablecast taped subject is important enough, then a timebase-correcting device will bring the home tape up to broadcast standards, thus eliminating the timebase problems.

Although several types of cable can carry video transmissions, *coaxial cable (coax)* is the most common for local applications. It consists of a conducting wire (usually copper) in the center encased in a dielectric insulator. Wrapped around this combination is a metallic braid, called the *shield* and still another, thicker outer insulator. Coax is made in many sizes from 1/8" to 1" in diameter.

In either a cable or a broadcast network, the camera and reception processes are pretty much the same. Actually, only the vehicle of transmission changes. More will be said about both "wire-less" transmission in the communications chapter.

RECEPTION

The home television functions basically like the video camera but in reverse (Figure 2–19). The incoming AM (video) and FM (audio) signals run from the antenna to an RF (radio frequency)

figure 2–19   A diagram of video reception.

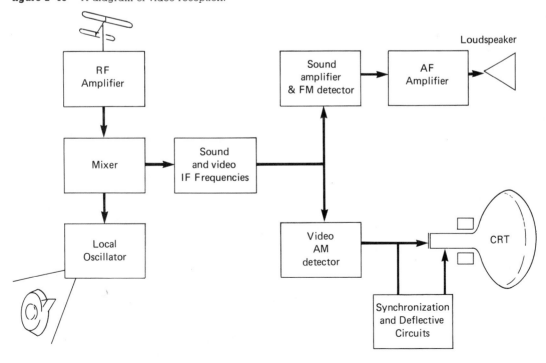

amplifier. The amplifier feeds the boosted signal to a *mixer*, which also receives a pulse from a built-in oscillator; the frequency of the oscillator is determined by the channel selector on the TV set. The oscillator *demodulates* the signal; simply stated, it turns the waves into varying levels of voltage. The resultant sound and video signals—the intermediate frequencies (IFs)—are then differentiated for forwarding to the loudspeaker and CRT (Figure 2–19). A *stable* picture results from the accurate tuning of the receiver to these incoming signals.

The Cathode Ray Tube (CRT). In a black-and-white CRT, the electron beam is directed onto the back of a phosphor-coated screen. The phosphors become illuminated when struck by the beam, their brightness determined by the intensity of the beam. Since the afterglow of these phosphors is about a sixtieth of a second, the molecular image should remain until the area is activated again by another scan. As in the video camera, the beam is controlled by deflection coils (Figure 2–20). While the beam speedily reconstructs the original image on the CRT screen, the viewer watches from the other side.

Color CRTs are only a little more complicated. Each of the phosphors glow in one of three colors: red, green, or blue. The

figure 2–20   The black-and-white cathode ray tube (CRT).

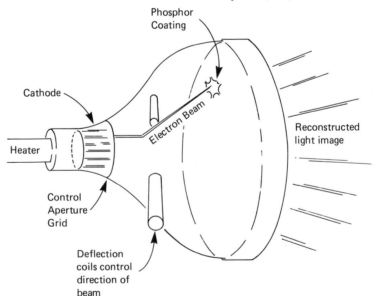

screen is actually a mosaic of red, green, and blue phosphor dots or bars. In viewer screens, each dot is surrounded by a black background that prevents the glow of one dot to meld with the others. The dots are arranged in tiers of one color each. A 21" screen may contain as many as 400,000 such groups.

The electron beam may be produced by either a single- or multiple-gun system. A single-gun system contains three "heater" cathodes for each of the three colors. In a three-gun set-up, each gun produces a single beam.

Between the gun and the screen is a *shadow mask*, which is an extremely thin sheet containing as many apertures (minute dots or bars) as there are trios on the screen. As the beam is shot through each aperture, it activates a set of color dots/bars. If the convergence of the three beams is perfect, the *purity* of the picture will be high. If the convergence is off, the color is not sharp and clear (Figure 2–21). In the United States, each

figure 2–21   The "color" beams pass through the aperture in the shadow mask.

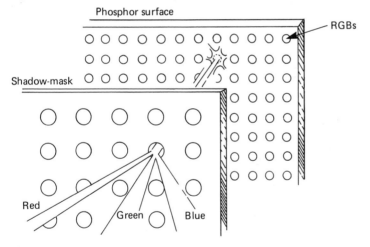

scan (or *frame*) consists of 525 horizontal lines. In other words, American TV pictures consist of 525 horizontal lines that are traced thirty times a second. In other countries, such as the PAL system in the United Kingdom or SECAM in Europe, 625 or 800 lines are standard. So in Figure 2–4, the horizontal traces, limited in number to six and exaggerated to demonstrate the principle, would actually be 525, 625, or 800, depending on where in the world the TV set is located. Obviously, the higher horizontal line counts indicate higher-quality pictures, but they also require a faster sync pulse. Moreover, the line count, or frame is one area in which the lack of standardization becomes evident.

Improvements in Video Transmission

That's the traditional video process in theory—the transmission and reception of color signals in a conventional broadcasting system. Obviously, the size of the screen is limited by the 525-line standard, but because it is the tried-and-true method, it is fairly well standardized. On a relatively small screen, 525 lines produces good resolution (or sharpness). Spread the same number of lines over a larger screen, and the resolution suffers. Yet even adding more lines to the screen does not permit an unlimited increase in the size of a CRT, because the electron beam can be manipulated to cover only a certain area in a given time frame. If the area becomes too large or the lines too many, the picture "flickers" because the afterglow does not cover the amount of time it takes the beam to reactivate the phosphor.

Nonetheless, many new and exciting experiments in TV tubes are bringing viewers larger and clearer pictures: higher line counts, improved circuitry controlling the beam, projection systems, and even whole new approaches to picture display that discard the CRT concept completely.

Picture Quality. In January of 1979, for example, Matsushita demonstrated a color television with vastly improved picture quality. The company's new "Miracle Mind" television contains an automatic white balancer and a special control circuit to ensure the purest and most stable white color possible. A new phosphor material on the screen generates truer colors. To further sharpen reception, the "Miracle Mind" has an intensely focused electron beam, a high-contrast picture screen, and a special cross-color eliminating circuit (see Figure 2–22).

figure 2-22   Matsushita's "Miracle" image TV.

Also in January of 1979, Matsushita revealed a 55″ diagonal television that is sharp, bright, and real. The "high-definition" color television system, which features dramatically improved sharpness and definition over conventional television reception, represents a major technological breakthrough that more than doubles resolution on the television screen, producing an unusually clear, realistic picture. The system is based on entirely new design concepts and utilizes 1,125 scanning lines, compared to the 525 in the standard television system. The crystal clarity and brilliance of the new system makes it especially suitable for projection TV, where high definition is essential. Fully developed, the system is available as a closed circuit system. But home users will have to wait until a new broadcast standard has been established (Figure 2-23).

Compact Screens.   Later in the year, manufacturers revealed other developments, especially in the area of compact screen.   63

figure 2–23   Matsushita's high-definition TV produces 1,125 scanning lines, with a horizontal frequency of 33.75 kHz and a vertical frequency of 60 Hz. Its aspect ratio is 3:5; and its color subcarrier frequency, 24.3 mHz.

Sanyo Corporation of America unveiled its Tri Screen TV—a 19″ color screen with an inset 2×5″ black-and-white screen. In connection with color cameras, the smaller screen can be used as a security monitor, while the larger screen displays broadcasts (see also Figure 2–49). Sharp revealed its research into a thin-film electroluminescent (EL) flat screen; its initial application was for inclusion as a 3″ black-and-white screen in a TV about the size of a paperback book. At the same time, General Telephone and Telegraph, in collaboration with Lucitron, Inc., announced that by 1981 it would make public a 50″ diagonal flat screen color display that operates on the principle of cathodoluminescence. This trend in developing flat video screens promises more than just smaller TVs for viewing; it reflects a trend toward merging with the development of plasma displays in computer hardware, discussed in Chapter 3.

3-D TV.   Perhaps most fascinating is the prospect of 3-D TV in your home. Also in 1979, Digital Optical Technology Systems of

figure 2–24 Matsushita's portable color TV eliminates the shadow mask from the picture tube and plays on batteries for longer periods than other battery sets. Like black-and-white sets, this one needs only one electron gun—which means it uses 40 percent less power and is far less bulky than previous portable color TV receivers. The new design replaces the conventional shadow mask on the screen with phosphors that give off ultraviolet light, which is used to control the electron beam.

figure 2–25 Users can "write" programs directly onto the screen of this TV/amusement center, by means of a light pen and an electronic color pallette at the base of the screen. Approximately 350 separate frames with sound can be recorded on a 60-minute audio cassette tape.

Amsterdam, in collaboration with Ancom Company of Scarsdale announced its work on a stereoptic color TV system that makes 3-D broadcasting a possibility. The system acts like a video computer that processes images *in digital form* to create the 3-D effect. (Yes, you have to wear special glasses.)

Now *that's* exciting!

Video Systems

Simply stated, a video system is a device that records both audio and video signals, either by direct connection to a TV antenna terminal or by a camera. Such a system usually includes some kind of playback capability, either on the TV screen or on a special monitor, as well as a camera, projection screen, or other optional devices. The storage medium may be either tape or disc:

1. *Videotape recorders* (Figure 2–26) are more often referred to as videocassette recorders (VCRs). They record via camera or television hook-up and play back on whatever type of regular or projection TV screen they are connected to. A video tape cassette looks and works very much like an audio tape cassette.

2. *Videodisc recorder/players* do the same thing, only the sights and sounds are stored on what looks like a record, a conventional LP (Figure 2–27). Generally, a disc holds two hours of program and with some systems an individual frame is accessed faster.

RECORDING ON TAPE

How does a video recorder capture images on tape? When the incoming composite video wave from the camera enters the video recorder, it is sent in two directions. First it goes to a synchronization separator, which calls out the vertical sync signal and amplifies it. From there, it goes to a frequency divider, which cuts the frequency of the remaining signal from 60 to 30 Hz. This halved signal passes through gate circuitry that goes to the timing of the reading head motor. Let's leave the signal there for a moment.

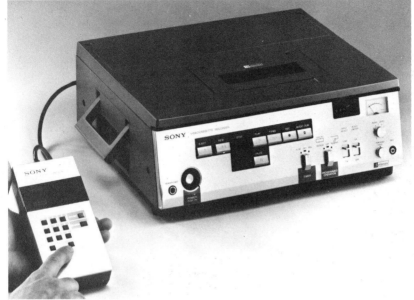

figure 2–26 (a) The Sony Betamax RM-300, using 1/2″ tape, plays from 30 to 60 minutes. Its features include remote control, automatic program operation, automatic search, anti-"jitter" stability, RF color modulator, stop-action, optical timer, automatic tape rewind, and anti-condensation ejection.

(b) The Sony SLO-320 has all the features of the 300, along with a manual audio gain control, a separate audio dub facility with a VU meter, as well as headphone and microphone inputs. It can record from a closed circuit or from the TV monitor.

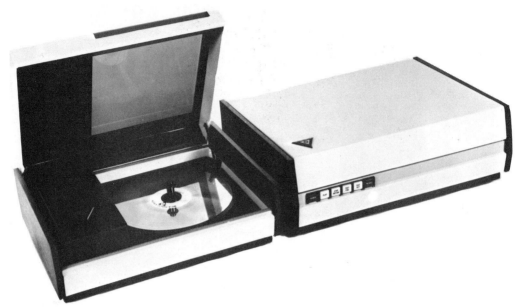

figure 2–27 (a) The Philips and MCA optical videodisc system, as shown, looks very much like a record player.

(b) A close-up of an MCA DiscoVision videodisc.

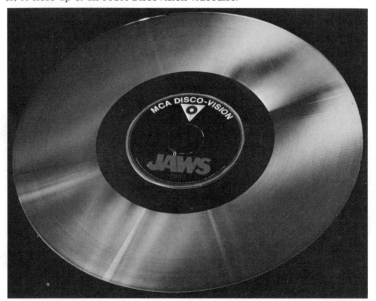

At the same time, the incoming composite signal is sent to a modulator and then to a booster. From the booster, the signal goes to the reading heads, where the halved vertical signal is controlling the speed of the reading heads (Figure 2–28).

As both signals enter the recording head, they are therefore coordinated. Half-inch tape (nonprofessional) recording drums contain two heads. Since the drum rotates at 30 rps (1,800 rpm) each head stays in contact with the tape for half a revolution—or the familiar sixtieth of a second. Vertical blanking takes place as the drum switches over from one head to the other.

figure 2–28   The incoming signal in the VTR.

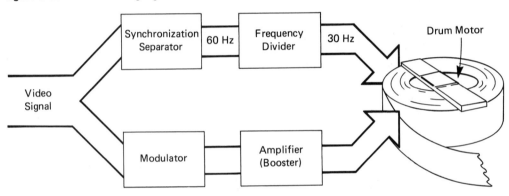

Each time a head records on the tape, it scans the width of the tape, which is moving (of course). The field of video information therefore consists of a diagonal "line" on the width of the tape (Figure 2–29). Hence the term *helical scan*. Each field, starting and ending within a vertical sync, prints 262.5 lines of horizontal information. Double that number, and you have 525—the number of lines required to construct a video image on an American TV set. Each head records half the picture. Thus the vertical sync pulse "times" the drum motor, to keep in rhythm with the composite signal fed from the booster. Together, they create a properly timed information field on the tape for later playback. Other important factors affect the quality of the recording—wear of the head, tape tension, treading control, among others—but the essence of video recording lies in this explanation.

69

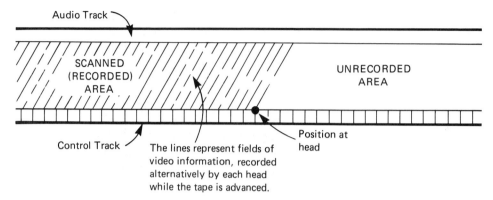

Audio Track

SCANNED
(RECORDED)
AREA

UNRECORDED
AREA

Control Track

Position at
head

The lines represent fields of
video information, recorded
alternatively by each head
while the tape is advanced.

figure 2-29 Pictorial representation of recorded tape.

Density. As popular as it is, video tape recording presents a problem. Since video signals carry so much electrical "information," the video storage surface has to cram a great number of electrical impulses into a given area. Video images therefore require great frequency response, and the tape must be extremely dense. Since videotape is very expensive, simply speeding up the recording process—for a higher-quality picture—would use up far too much tape and make the cost of the tape cassette prohibitive.

The problem was partially solved by increasing the reading/recording speed by rotating the video recording heads. Most VCRs have the dual recording heads mounted on opposite sides of a drum that have already been described. The helical scanning technique made tape utilization more efficient.

The problem was all but eliminated with the advent of 1/2″ tape, to replace the 3/4″ tape used in earlier systems. The narrower tape records at a slower speed, and recording a program therefore consumes less tape, as little as one-seventh as much as the wider tape.

In mid-1979, Phillips/Grundig further confused the multistandard video recorder market by starting production on a 1/4″ recorder—the VR 2020. Actually it utilizes a 1/2″ tape, which consists of two 1/4″ tracks running side by side. With this greater compactness, the playing time increases to 4 hours—for *each* track. The system also features a self-correcting system for video heads, called the "dynamic track following" (DTF) system. A set of inscriptions on the tape, made during recording, acts as a control signal for the replay. It also, says its maker, makes the tapes more interchangeable among machines.

Longitudinal Video Recorders. In another approach to "packing" more density onto the tape surface, manufacturers are returning to *longitudinal-scan video recorders* (LVRs), sometimes known as "fixed-head recorders." Whereas in helical scanning, the reading head bobs up and down to read the diagonally recorded signal on the tape (Figure 2–29), the reading head in an LVR remains in one position because it reads the tape in a straight line end to end. When the head comes to the end of the tape, it switches down to the next track in a matter of milliseconds, while the tape reverses direction to be read the other way.

Manufacturers are "returning" to this playback method because the idea is not a new one. In the 1960s, SONY came up with an open-reel recorder that used 1/2" tape, and it followed up with the U-matic, which used a 3/4" tape cassette. Now BASF of Germany, Matsushita and Toshiba of Japan, RCA and Magnovox of America among others—are all reevaluating the merits of LVR. Some popular models promise to cost as little as $500.

figure 2–30 The Vidstar video home system (CRU-8300U) is an electronic color editing videocassette recorder/player. Using a 1/2" tape, JVC's rotary erase head traces the video track helically.

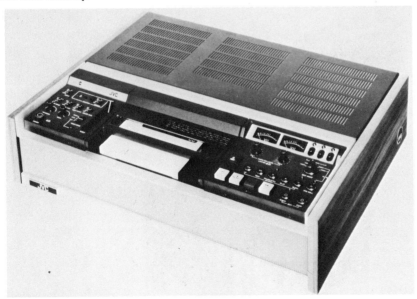

Courtesy: Japan Victor Corporation

figure 2–31   Akai's Activideo system is a VHS-format home VCR that is easily transported for use with any TV system in the house. For that matter, it operates on either AC current or rechargeable car/boat batteries.

figure 2–32   The Sony HVC-1000 portable color camera, the SL-3000 portable Betamax, and the TT-3000 Tuner-Timer allow users to record or to shoot "tapies" almost anywhere.

figure 2–33 Panasonic's portable 2-hour/4-hour Omnivision IV VHS recorders (PV-2100 and PV-2200) employ versatile two-piece design and a three-way power operation (AC, DC, car battery). Each has two sections—a self-contained, battery-operated player/recorder and a tuner/digital timer.

figure 2–34   Toshiba's improved version of the endless-loop, fixed-head LVR was first shown in prototype form in June, 1979. Its playing time is 2 hours, doubled from the original 1 hour. The track system is 300 (up from 220). Its chief advantage is its fast access time—8.4 seconds to scan from track number 1 to track number 300, at a rate of 0.03 second from one track to another.

Which Standard Is Standard?   Confusion among consumers causes some to hesitate because of the two different formats. The EIAJ has established two formats as "standard": (1) the B or Beta and (2) the Video Home System (VHS). In the Beta category, the primary manufacturers are Sony, Toshiba, Zenith, RCA, Magnavox, Japan Victor Corporation (JVC) and its parent, Matsushita Electric (Figure 2–35), along with many others.

Distinctions between the two systems do *not* affect the camera you use, but they do affect the type of CRT you use. Although both differ in technical detail, they both use 1/2″ tape. Neither of these systems should be confused with the Sony U-Matic 3/4″ or with the broadcast-quality 1″ or 2″ helical scan open-reel tapes. (Incidentally, neither the 1″ nor 2″ tapes require splitting of the image into y, I, Q signals before transmission.) In this book, we refer exclusively to the 1/2″ Beta or VHS formats. The many manufacturers of video equipment are shown in Table 2–3.

The reading head poses another standardization problem. The Electronics Industries Association (EIA) sets the standards for American manufacturers. The specific standard of 525 lines per frame for domestic TVs was established by the National Television Standards Committee (NTSC). But since so much video equipment is made in Japan, the EIA of Japan (EIAJ) dominates the standard-setting. So while the EIA has over the years established compatability in the American video broadcasting industry, the EIAJ is introducing equipment whose synchronization pulses are slightly off from American equipment.

Which One Is for You? In connection with these different types of systems, home users have to bear in mind their own personal levels of knowledge and ability. Most 1/2" tape units are easily installed by the nontechnical user according to instructions in

figure 2–35   This device duplicates 2- or 4-hour VHS tapes in volume. Whereas conventional duplicators requires as much time as the regular running time of the original, this model duplicates by means of magnetic transfer—in just 5 minutes.

Courtesy: Matsushita

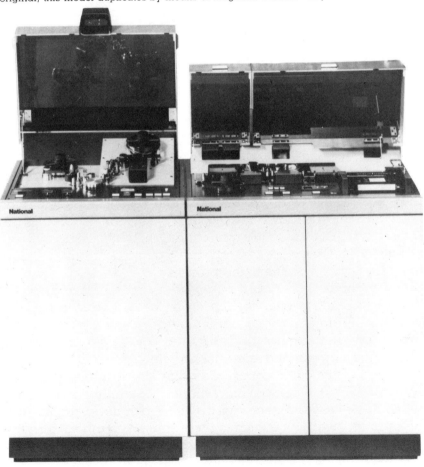

Table 2–3. *Video system manufacturers*

Brand	Format	Mfr.
Admiral		(indefinite)
Aiwa	Beta-2	Sony
Akai	VHS	Akai
GE	VHS-4	Matsushita
Hitachi	VHS-2	Hitachi
JVC	VHS-2	JVC
Magnavox	VHS-4	Matsushita
C. Mathes	VHS-4	Matsushita
MGA	VHS-2	JVC
M. Ward	VHS-4	RCA-Matsushita
Panasonic	VHS-4	Matsushita
Pioneer	Beta-2	Sony
Quasar	VX-2000	Matsushita
RCA	VHS-4	Matsushita
Sanyo	V-Cord II	Sanyo
	Beta-2	Sanyo
Sears	Beta-2	Sanyo
Sharp	VHS-2	JVC
Sony	Beta-2	Sony
Sylvania	VHS-4	Matsushita
Toshiba	Beta-2	Sony
Zenith	Beta-2	Sony
B-H/BASF	New	Bell&Howell

the manual. The 3/4" systems, however, involve electronic incompatabilities with the TV set; as a result, a professional should install the device. Of course, the 1" or 2" broadcast-quality systems require the type of training that most nonprofessionals do not have. Unless you are technically trained, leave 2" (quadruplex) systems to the pros.

Most home VCRs do not require a special video monitor, as professional systems do. Once connected to a standard TV through the antenna terminals, they are completely self-contained. Users need only the blank videocassettes to make it go, and a videocamera and microphone (which is usually attached) to do their own productions. Cameras do not suffer from the same problems in compatibility that recorder/players do. Automatic timer/programmers can set the machine to record any program at any hour, switch to programmed channels, turn the recorder on and off appropriately, and do this for periods of up to a week on one programmed setting.

How It Works. If tape is versatile and easily modified, then videodiscs are capacious, economical, high-quality, and rugged. Though the disc resembles a long-playing record and is pressed like one, the similarities end there. Whereas a record is played by a chisel-like stylus in a groove, the latest discs are cut by lasers and played through an electronic stylus. In recording, a laser beam is split in two: One signal records the video (or audio) information, while the other provides an electronic "track" for the stylus to follow later in playback (Figure 2–36). The information signal creates variable pits on the disc surface, the tracking signal creates lines or playback pits. Both signals are picked up as electronic capacitance variations between the disc and the electrode on the stylus. Since the grooves are "imaginary," the stylus never actually touches the

figure 2–36 The stylus.

Courtesy: Japan Victor Corporation

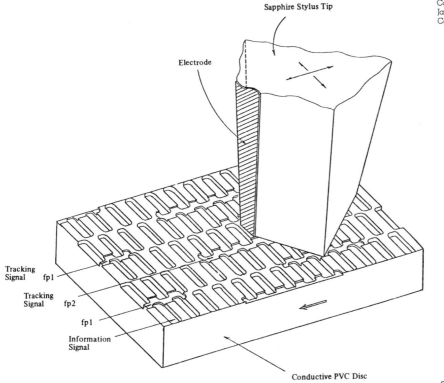

Sapphire Stylus Tip

Electrode

Tracking Signal   fp1

Tracking Signal   fp2

fp1

Information Signal

Conductive PVC Disc

disc. Instead it moves fully over the electro-conductive disc surface (Figure 2–37). Once the signal is picked up from the disc surface, it is broken down in its video and audio components before routing to the screen and loudspeaker. Thus the laser solves the problems of distortion, wear, tear, density, economy, and durability.

figure 2–37 The operation of the stylus is electromagnetic.

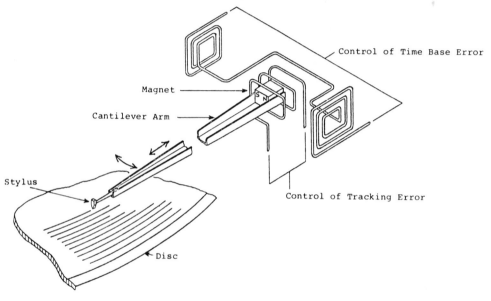
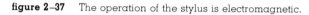

Courtesy: Japan Victor Corporation

Drawbacks. As the laser solved those problems, it created others. One is standardization. Any conventional LP can now be played on any conventional record player; the standardization of the records and players took years of cooperation among the industry's manufacturers. With so many manufacturers entering the videodisc market, the question arises as to whether the discs put out by one company will be playable on another company's player.

Another drawback is that, practically speaking, the disc is not user-programmable: the video information can be recorded only at the factory. However, even so, a one-copy mastering technique has been developed that allows the institutional user to make up a relatively inexpensive master disc—without com-

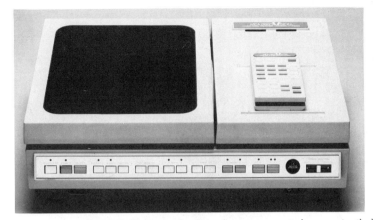

figure 2–38 The MCA-Philips' videodisc player is operated conveniently by the hand-held remote control terminal, which also provides the user with many other functions.

Courtesy: MCA-Philips

plicated processing or developing. The single disc produced for the laser system user has the same characteristics and advantages of the mass-produced disc. Thus the laser disc can be programmed for such automatic operations as random access, start and stop, freeze-frame, fast or slow display, and reverse action.

figure 2–39 RCA's videodisc player, the SFT100, is so simple to use that anyone can use it right out of the shipping carton. Two-hour playing time per disc, forward and reverse visual search, rapid access, pause control, and microcomputer control are all standard features, among others.

Courtesy: RCA

figure 2–40   With RCA's SelectaVision, the disc is taken automatically from its jacket directly into the turntable—never touched by the user's hands.

Advantages.   Perhaps the most outstanding feature of the laser videodisc is its huge storage capacity. Initially each side played only thirty minutes of video programming, while the lower-cost mechanical discs recorded up to two hours. Used exclusively for audio recording, a laser disc plays up to fifteen hours of recorded music; as such, it can replace Muzak-type services. Or consider this: All the pages of the *Encyclopedia Britannica* and all its annual supplements could be stored on one disc— with room to spare! Up to 400 million nine-digit numbers, such as Social Security numbers, can be stored three times over on one such disc; in other words, if at some future time the population of the United States increased to roughly six times its present size, everyone's Social Security number could be preserved on only one laser-type videodisc!

Another advantage is the disc's easy access: For instance, the user who stores TV programs on a disc can lock onto any of the 54,000 frames per side for precise and easy cueing. And each frame may be identified on a viewing screen by means of a digital display. Selection of any frame is nearly instantaneous.

A laser disc is also a dirt-cheap computer storage medium. For a 60¢ manufacturing copy cost, each of the 54,000 frames costs roughly one ten thousandth of one cent. Considering that each side actually contains something in the neighborhood of 540 billion bits of information, the economics become even more convincing.

This dense, high-quality, low-cost storage medium is also rugged enough to survive mailing anywhere for almost any purpose: Discs can be mailed to branch stores for credit verification, price updating or marketing communication. X-rays can be transferred en masse from one hospital to another. Blocks of instruction and training can be shipped simultaneously to all parts of governmental organizations all over the country or the world. Previously cumbersome microfilm files can now be transported cheaply on a single disc. Given the mass marketing and standardization of the appropriate hardware, videodiscs can be used in any number of ways.

We will say more about disc storage and its many applications in the next chapter. For now, suffice it to say that the disc's lack of compatibility among video recorder/players has apparently failed to dampen the buying public's enthusiasm. In 1979, a Japanese study group predicted that the demand for these units—in whatever form—in the United States alone will grow from 575,000 in 1978 to 2.1 million by 1983! Hence the economic incentive for manufacturers endeavors.

Mixers

Video *mixers (switchers)* enable a video recorder or CRT to "switch" from one input to another, thus "mixing" their effects. The technical name for these devices is *special effects generators (SEGs)*. They perform a variety of functions in the video field alone, usually switch from the input of one camera to that of another as both cameras feed a single monitor (Figure 2–41). The basic requirement is that all inputs (in this case, cameras) must be synchronized. If the SEG attempts to switch from one input to another while one is at the end of a field and the other is in the middle, a "flash" appears.

TYPES OF MIXING

Switching. The screen can switch from one input to another, smoothly, as long as the two inputs are synchronized. If they are not, a time-delay device has to hold up on one input until the next one is in a blanking period. Switches can be made during either horizontal or vertical blanking periods.

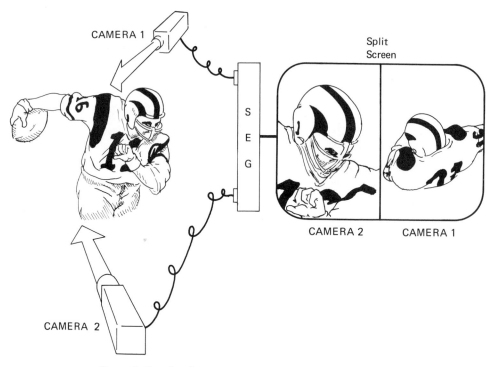

CAMERA 1

Split
Screen

S
E
G

CAMERA 2   CAMERA 1

figure 2–41   A split screen.

Fading.   To fade out of one input and into another, the SEG
lowers the voltage of the outgoing input from full to zero, while
simultaneously raising the voltage of the incoming voltage from
zero to full. (Figure 2–42).

figure 2–42   A fade.

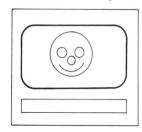

Outgoing Input at 100%

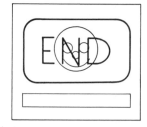

Outgoing and Incoming
Inputs Both at 50%

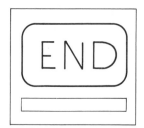

Outgoing Input is 0%;
Incoming Input is 100%.

Split-Screen. The screen can be split several different ways: horizontally, vertically (Figure 2–41), or diagonally. In a horizontal split, part of the horizontal scanning time is assigned to one input; the balance is assigned to another. Vertical splits are handled the same way. In a diagonal split, the assignment of times to the successive horizontal scans is complicated but done.

Wiping. A wipe is nothing more than a split screen in which the line of demarcation between the two images is moving. A diagonal wipe is called a corner insert. (Figure 2–43).

figure 2–43   Wiping—corner insert.

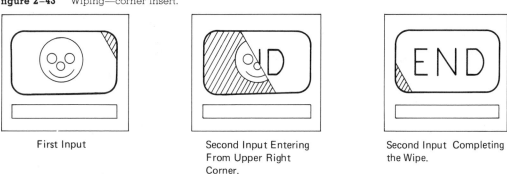

First Input   Second Input Entering From Upper Right Corner.   Second Input Completing the Wipe.

Negative Image. Simply by reversing the voltages of the lights and darks, the image is reversed: The blacks become white, and the whites become black.

Genlock. A genlock capability permits an SEG to combine a prerecorded image with camera input of a live subject (Figure 2–44).

figure 2–44   Genlock.

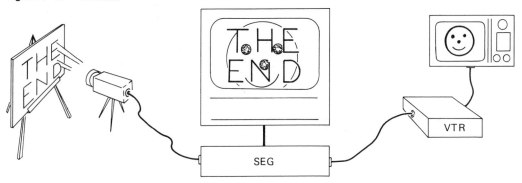

Matting. This effect consists of fitting a subject against a background other than the one actually there. For instance, newscasters are sometimes shown seated at a desk, behind which a riot scene is taking place. The riot scene was taped earlier in the day and fed into the SEG, while the camera feeds the image of the newscaster. The subject usually is placed against a background that "drops out," that is, one that is not picked up by video cameras or one that can be filtered out with a lens attachment.

figure 2–45 Sophisticated video tape editing can be performed on RCA's AE-600 time code editing system. Such a system must be considered "institutional," but it demonstrates what the control console of such a system looks like.

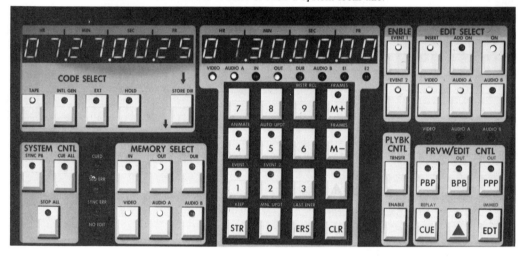

Courtesy: RCA

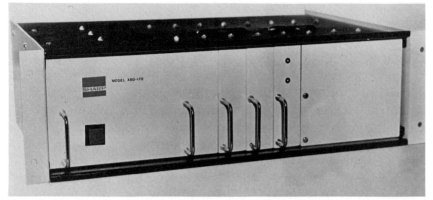

Courtesy:
Sharp Electronics
Corporation

figure 2–46 Sharp's color sync generator with a built-in phase shifter accommodates three cameras and black background generator. The configuration (XSG-170) is completely modular, allowing the user to add accessories, including a color bar generator, phase module for two additional cameras, and an audio test oscillator. It carries a suggested user net price of $775.

THE MIXER ITSELF

Inside the SEG or sometimes as a separate unit is a *synchronization* generator, a device that coordinates the timing of all the inputs. On the SEG is a panel of switches connected to buses on the inside, which enable the user to mix and switch images.

Brushing aside momentarily the differences between the outputs of computers and video recorders, the mixer is a critical and valuable component of the video computer. If the inputs can be properly demodulated and synchronized, data and video information can be combined in an unlimited number of fascinating ways. We will pursue this subject in the next chapter.

Projection Systems

High-quality television projection systems approach the ultimate in home viewing. If video presentations needed any additional visual dramatic impact, these systems have it.

In the projection-system market, two camps have formed up. One consists of the $2,000 to $3,000 high-quality systems by Advent, MGA (Mitsubishi), Sony, GE, and a few others. The other camp is comprised of the less expensive, $300 to $1,800 systems; some of these attach to 11″ to 19″ portable TVs, either color or black-and-white, while others can be bellowed for projection onto larger screens that fold back when not in use.

Many cheap plastic magnifying imitations of high-quality units are flooding the market. Some kits, for $250 to $300 are actually good values, but you must know which ones they are. Kits can be risky purchases: Some honest dealers clearly state that from ten to fifteen hours are required to build the systems and that the purchaser must supply the necessary particle board, formica, or furniture-quality lumber, as well as the 12″ to 19″ portable TV.

Also, many people who see a large projected video image for the first time might be so overwhelmed that they might make a hasty purchase. However, wide differences in quality, even among models by the same manufacturer, make a purchase decision especially difficult. These differences in picture quality, in display flexibility, in added control capabilities, and the like are particularly important for commercial, industrial, or institutional users.

So be especially wary and investigative if you are considering the purchase of a projection system.

THE LOW-PRICED SYSTEMS

Kits. Included in kits are usually a set of plans, a special lens, two mirrors (one typically 8″ × 10″ and the other, 14 3/4″ × 20″) and a 32″ × 40″/50″ (diagonal) screen. When constructed according to the directions, the device consists of a self-contained internal projection TV that uses the portable TV and requires about 2′ × 4′ of floor space.

Bellows. One fully constructed bellows type, very similar to the old fold-up camera, is available with 56″- to 6′-diameter screens. Fastened to the back of a TV screen, the bellows guard the image from outside light. The bellows with an adjustable cradle for TV, allows the maximum amount of light and detail to reach the rear projection 38″ × 40″ screen. The user can increase or decrease the size and intensity of the picture by moving the screen-lens system in or out from the unit. The systems, factory-built, sell for under $200.

THE MID-PRICED SYSTEMS

From these simpler systems, customers can move up the mid-price range of about $900 to $1,600. Muntz has many dealers advertising its Home Theater Television. Eastman Kodak's 30″ × 40″ screen, about four times larger than the average TV screen, is often part of a typical system. A self-contained unit in a furniture-like cabinet, it is essentially a Sony 15″ color portable TV with a Trinitron picture tube. The image is projected with a Muntz precision ground German lens and mirror system, which directs the picture onto the Ektalite screen. Prices from $1,395 to $1,795, are expected to fall rapidly with volume sales.

Another system is Projection Television's Video series. These units include a 7″, FL 45 lens system with a washable screen. Viewing may take place under normal lighting conditions. An acoustic suspension sound system and full audio-video inputs are included in the product. The Video series also includes a combination VCR-projection unit, a complete interconnection between the projection TV and the VCR, that features a two-hour recording capability. The small projection set, Model 2000, is priced at $1,050; and the large 6′-foot system, Model 4000, costs $1,250. The VCR combination projection units are available at just over $2,000.

THE HIGH-PRICED SYSTEMS

The market for the $2,000 to $3,000 systems is a little complicated. Many companies, all over the world, have products either on the drawing boards, in production, or on the store shelves. Advent was the initial leader, though GE was one of the few large American TV manufacturers that entered the game early. Several major Japanese firms entered the projection business in late 1978 and throughout 1979. Mitsubishi (MGA Figure 2–47) offers its two-piece Video Scan System (VSS), with a 6′ screen, for under $3,000. And Panasonic (Matsushita) developed a three-tube system in a one-piece furniture unit. Also, Sharp is demonstrating its three-tube system in Japan, eventually to distribute it widely throughout the United States. Sony, not to be left out of the business, offers several units, including a one-tube projector that has been available for years. Their line now 87

figure 2–47   The Mitsubishi Video Scan System is a two-part set-up: (1) Screen Model VE-700U—The 6′ durable and washable screen is highly reflective, making its brightness very good. It is large enough for most commercial uses, but it is also small enough for home use. (2) Projector Model VS-700U—The projector contains three CRTs with six-function veractor turning and remote control, an active convergence system, and video jacks for VCR and video camera connections. The speakers are aimed toward the screen to give the illusion that the sound emanates from the image.

includes models in multiple-tube configurations. GE, too, is marketing its consumer system priced under $3000 to grab a significant segment of an apparently ever-expanding universe of big-screen program projection. Panasonic has shown some dealers a three-tube system designed in a one-piece cabinet with a screen 5' in diameter. Finally, Projecta-Vision promotes their system as being the first truly portable projection TV. This unit features an RCA 15" XL-100 color TV and a Kodak Ektalite screen in three sizes and prices.

In high-priced systems, however, two companies dominate the sales: Advent and GE.

Advent. The big jump ahead was made by the Advent Corporation of Cambridge, Massachusetts. Advent's VideoBeam Model 710 can be used in small rooms or viewed by up to two hundred people in an auditorium. For larger groups of up to four hundred or more, a simple inexpensive adapter modifies the VideoBeam TV projector to provide a 6' × 8' (10' diagonal) picture for film-like viewing in a darkened theater or lecture hall. A simple approach to projecting a large, clear picture for

figure 2–48   Advent's Model 760 is a two-piece television consisting of a new, low-profile projector console that projects the picture from regular TV broadcasts or a videocassette player to a separate 6' diagonal screen. The Model 760's picture is twice the size and has five times the brightness of one-tube projection sets, and it is eight times larger than the 25" set.

daylight viewing, is to collect the light from a conventional direct-view color picture tube by means of a lens placed in front of the tube. A major difficulty with this approach is that the tube's light output has already been reduced by four-fifths by the shadow mask which separates the color phosphors. Collecting a high percentage of the remaining light requires a large and optically fast—hence *very* expensive—lens; such a lens is not economically feasible. Therefore, to increase the available light the tube is often driven to a level which sacrifices tube life and increases spot size, degrading picture quality.

To achieve the desired combination of size, brightness, and clarity with available technology requires the use of three individual tube/lens systems. This is the approach Advent took

figure 2–48

Courtesy: Advent

in first developing VideoBeam television. The use of three tubes eliminates that prime limiter of color tube efficiency, the shadow mask, resulting in a substantial increase in brightness without reducing tube life nor increasing spot size, a particularly important consideration with the high image magnification involved. Furthermore, the three projection tubes permit the efficient use of relatively large lenses, which are not only comparatively inexpensive, but which also project a large percentage of the tubes' light to the screen. Finally, the use of three tubes eliminates the phosphor dots or stripes of the direct view color tube, patterns that can be visually annoying when blown up to such a large size.

Forming the other end of the closed VideoBeam television system is its special projection screen, developed to play a vital role in the system's overall performance. The screen, first of all, provides very high reflectivity, with a gain on axis of at least 10, to waste as little as possible of the projector's light output. The screen also has a directional and differentially reflecting property, to concentrate the light from the projector into the viewing area, and as an equally beneficial corollary, to reject ambient light reaching the screen from off-axis. As a result, VideoBeam television need not be viewed in full darkness, as long as sources of room lighting are located off axis. Because of its high gain, the screen is shaped to a carefully calculated spherical section, to provide uniform brightness within its wide viewing angle.

VideoBeam television's three-tube projection system and special projection screen provide a television picture large enough and bright enough to make a significant difference in the way people relate to it, and to make the added cost in dollars and living space worthwhile. The optical system also insures "high fidelity" performance characteristics that do justice to the enormously revealing picture. At the same time, these goals are achieved with surprising cost and energy efficiencies. The three 5" color tubes and 5" lenses are not only economical to manufacture, but also provide enough picture brightness to accommodate the different ambient light levels preferred for movie and television viewing. At the same time, overall power consumption of Advent's 5', 6', and 7' sets is comparable to that of today's solid-state 25" sets, and far less than that of tube color sets of a few years ago.

Anyone who has used a regular color TV set can operate a VideoBeam TV set without special training. No technician, projectionist, or audio-visual expert is required. Neither do you have to wait for warm-up, as the set has instant-on operation. The VideoBeam system (Figure 2–48) can also display images from a wide variety of signal sources, including:

—Videotape, from 1/2″ cassettes to 2″ quad
—Most camera films, both color and monochrome
—Computer interface devices
—Super 8 film video players
—Character generators
—Closed-circuit, multi-point distribution systems
—Off-air broadcasts with a built-in UHF-VHF tuner
—Cable TV
—Image intensifiers
—X-ray interface devices
—Video synthesizers and games
—New developments, such as videodisc players and commercial satellite receivers

Thousands of VideoBeam sets are in use, and dealers report high sales. The Model 1000A Remote Control, with picture tuning controls in a compact control unit, connects to the projector via a 30′ cable that extends to 90′. The picture is claimed to be at least ten times larger than that of a conventional TV monitor. The model consists of a receiver/projector screen that may be wall-mounted. The color picture is projected onto the screen by means of three patented LightGuide® projection tubes. Sound is also projected to and reflected back from the screen, by a high-fidelity sound system built into the front of the projector.

General Electric. GE's first large-screen projection system, the Model PJ5000, is an institutional system, designed for the display of financial and computer information to large audiences. However, since several publications have reported on the GE models for personal use, we might as well take a look at the PJ5000.

Courtesy:
Quasar Electronics
Company

figure 2–49   Quasar's projection TV incorporates a 5' screen of washable Ektalite. The unit can be remotely controlled with direct access to all 82 channels.

Like other projection systems, GE's produces instant, dynamic recall. GE has stressed its capability with computer output. For example, images from computer data banks, financial and investment statistics, advertising data, training material, or stockholders reports can be presented on a large color screen. Coupled to computer facilities through suitable interface equipment, it can project alphanumeric data, graphic displays, and computer-generated images in real time. In addition, it can project information from all standard video sources such as an off-air TV tuner, videotape, videocassette, videodisc, live camera, closed-circuit data network, or video film chain. It also has a simple remote control device.

The Widescreen 1000 is GE's consumer unit. Priced at about $2,800, it is a single-tube system in a one-piece cabinet, with a 45.7' diagonal screen that is flat and washable. The special 13" picture tube, developed especially for the projection unit, has an electron gun and mask, as well as two concealed mirrors that reflect the image. The screen consists of a diffuser that creates the image the viewer sees and a fresnel lens that gathers and shapes light for additional brightness. Other features include a broadcast controlled color tuning system, electronic tuning, and random access remote control.

Others.   Naturally, Mitsubishi is not to be left out of this ground-floor market. Its Video Scan System, for both commercial and consumer sales, runs about $3,400, but it is distributed (through Melco Sales, Inc.) only to dealers who guarantee proper demonstration that this model apparently warrants. Quasar's 5' self-contained projection system (see Figure 2–47), available in late 1978, features an Ektalite screen, touch-tuning, and the first use of a microprocessor in a projection TV tuning system. The audio is quadraphonic. Panasonic also puts out a one-piece 60" system, with a three-speaker system, for about $3,000.

Summary

Video equipment has taken such strides in the past few years that it is hard to keep pace with it. You can see, however, that the video elements for an integrated video computer are either available or in development. In the next chapter, we will view the system from a computerist's point of view—and deal with some of the issues in the construction of an IVT.

chapter **3**

The Computerist's
Point of View

The personal computer phenomenon grows out of many trends. Several decades ago, transistor radios demonstrated how convenient an electronic device could be. More recently, electronic calculators gradually became more portable, more programmable, and *less* costly. And within the past few years, video games stepped over from the boardwalk arcades into living rooms, and rather quickly they became not computerized games but computers that played games. Within a few years, computers were "personalized." Today the home computer market is like a fireworks display: Apples, Ataris, Ballys, Intellivisions, and many, many others are flooding the market.

Primarily as a result of this nontechnical avenue of approach, many people have come to think that the home television set is the same as a computer monitor.

That assumption is not totally correct. While the TV was designed simply to receive modulated radio frequencies, the computer display must accept output from a computer processor. Hence a home TV requires all incoming signals to be carried in on radio frequency (RF)—that is, fundamentally analog—signals. Before the video game can be displayed, the data from the cartridge or chip has to be mixed with an RF signal as it enters the TV set (Figure 3–1). The ingoing signal is thus "modulated" to resemble an incoming broadcast or cable signal. A true computer monitor, however, accepts data from the "computer" part of a system directly. Conversely, a computer monitor, constructed to accept digital signals from a central processor, simply does not recognize analog RF signals.

Even so, the TV suffices for many but not all computer applications—especially when users have to view the screen at close range for long periods of time. When the integrated video terminal is complete, the CRT must meet stricter specifications than the home TV tube can cope with at its present state of development. In the last chapter, we saw how a home television system operates. In this chapter, let's compare that process with a computer terminal's operation.

The Crossover
From Games To Computers

The misconception that a TV serves as a ubiquitous monitor seems to have come about as a result of the video game craze. The conversion of the television screen from a vehicle of passive

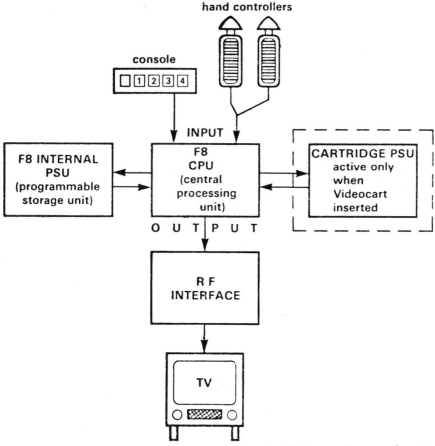

hand controllers

console

Courtesy: Fairchild Camera and Instruments Corporation

figure 3–1   An operations diagram of the (now discontinued) Channel F system. Note the RF interface.

entertainment to one of active participation camouflaged its unsuitability for more sophisticated computer applications.

As games became more popular, they became more "programmable." Games came with more cartridges, cassettes, or some other form of plug-in variations. The basic console became a vehicle for an ongoing line of games rather than a toy by itself: APF, Atari, Bally, Intellivision by Mattel, and others slowly edged their way toward entry into the computer business.

All of these programmables actually "crossed over" to become home/personal computers. This tendency was latent in the early microprocessor games with their computer-like capabilities, and it gradually became evident as these games acquired more and more programmable features and peripherals. Many good examples are on the store shelves today.

97

Bally. The Home Library Computer is a good example of this crossover, since it is an outgrowth of Bally's Arcade video games. The Bally unit, with its powerful Z-80 microprocessor, has a 4K RAM and an 8K ROM with three built-in games. It also has built-in calculator routines that display themselves on the owner's TV from the ten-memory calculator. Extras consist of a multi-color pen, a music-synthesizer, add-on board, two information-filing systems (one for insurance purposes, the other for phone numbers), a modem as an interface allowing Bally owners to communicate and exchange data, 16K RAM memory expansion, and a high-speed printer. Users can draw directly on the TV screen with an optional electronic wand in thirty-two different colors and in eight shades of each color. They can also compose, record, and play back music on an electronic synthesizer. They can store their personal records. They can play chess on the phone with other players, watching the moves on the TV. Some "game"!

Intellivision. In January of 1979, Mattel put Intellivision—another good "for-instance"—into the mass market (Figure 3–2). It is

figure 3-2   Mattel's Intellivision

Courtesy: Mattel

a home and game computer system that includes two separately purchased components: the master entertainment component and the keyboard. The entertainment console contains a 16-bit microprocessor and various interface chips that provide a 60 × 92 line graphics configuration, a 16-color pallet, and a three-part harmony musical synthesis. Also included are two hand-held controllers that each feature a 12-button keyboard; a unique, sixteen direction object control disc, and four separate action buttons. The computer add-on module consists of a typewriter keyboard, a magnetic tape drive under microprocessor control, a microphone, various memory and interface chips and parts for added hardware components. The software is sold in "networks." Some networks are sold in the form of ROM cartridges, and it can be utilized with the entertainment console and computer add-on module combined. In early 1981, Mattel was on the cutting edge of the game-turned-computer market.

Atari. In early 1979, this firm introduced two new personal computer systems developed for people with no prior computer experience but with a need for computer capability: The Atari-400[tm] Personal Computer (the general-purpose system) and the Atari-800[tm] Personal Computer (a specialized system). The Atari line includes a substantial library of computer software consisting of applications such as Personal Financial Management, Income Tax Preparation, Household and Office Record Keeping, Computer Aided Instruction in over 20 subject areas, including Math, English, History, Literature, Economics, Psychology, Auto Mechanics, and many others. Atari also offers a sophisticated series of action and thinking games for one to four players. The Atari Program Library is continuously expanded by a full-time staff of professional programmers.

Atari computers also contain custom integrated circuits for superior color graphics display, superior sound and music synthesis, slots for instantaneous use of preprogrammed solid-state cartridges and compatibility with a custom tape recorder for program storage and retrieval. UL approved, they connect directly to a standard color or black-and-white television. Both systems are programmable by the user.

figure 3–3 The Atari 800 (a) is a full-fledged home computer, as can be seen from the array of software and peripherals that are becoming available (b).

Sinclair. The ZX80 is an indicator of things to come and certainly at least the partial fulfillment of a prediction. That prediction was made by Sinclair Research's VP Nigel Searle in December of 1980: "In the 1980's we'll see a personal computer evolution similar to the development of calculators during the 1970's. In 1970, calculators were heavy desk machines used by accountants, and today, there's one built into my watch. Computers are next." The marvelous things about the ZX80 are its size—6.5" × 8.5" × 1.5"—and its weight—only 12 ounces. Despite these minikin proportions, it does everything that larger, more expensive home computers do.

Nor is that all. Implied in Searle's announcements are such things as the integration of ZX80 with photograph-sized screens (for great portability) and with large data banks (such as those available from Viewdata-like systems). Access by voice rather than by keyboard is also on Sinclair's agenda.

figure 3–4   The Sinclair ZX80, the world's lowest priced computer at $199.95, utilizes a standard home television screen for display, and a tape cassette recorder for program storage. In January, 1981, Sinclair Research Limited introduced a 16K memory expansion module for the existing unit.

Courtesy: Sinclair Research Ltd.

APF Electronics. APF's Imagination Machine is a home computer system that reflects on evolution of APF's video game expertise (Figure 3–5). Utilizing the home TV set as an output unit, the system contains a full keyboard, special numeric pad, joysticks, tape cassette storage (which allows audio recording for special talk/sound effects to programs), full 8-color graphics, and software designed along broad lines.

figure 3–5 APF Electronics' personal computer, THE IMAGINATION MACHINE will keep track of your home finances for a balanced budget which suits your needs and helps you plan for the future.

Courtesy: APF Electronics, Inc.

Why all the jawing about video games? The answer is, quite simply, because they demonstrate in a concrete way the close breeding between games that many people love to play and the home computers that many people have and that many more people would like to have. So they represent not only the blurred distinction between the types of displays, but also their increasing popularity among nontechnical users—hobbyists, homemakers, students, children, and the like.

The Problem
With TVs

These computers (a.k.a. video games) leave us with some good news and some bad news. The good news is that they make maximum use of the existing personal terminal—the TV set. By reducing the amount of "hardware" that the consumer has to purchase, game makers position their products within most people's "buying horizon." Additionally, watching the "good ole" TV light up with stick figures, game boards, and other entertainment features makes the user's adjustment to an unfamiliar product all the easier. The bad news is that, to take the next step toward a true computer terminal, manufacturers have to get around the analog–digital problem. Should all signals entering the TV be modulated for acceptability? Or should the set be modified to accept only digital signals or digital and analog signals?

The likely applications for an IVT call for some sort of solution to this problem, because the screen on such a system must be capable of simultaneously displaying the two essentially different types of information:

1. *Video (analog) information*, which may be live subjects shot through a camera, subjects from other media (slides, tapes, discs, etc.) or subjects from broadcasting or cable networks.
2. *Data (digital) display*, which may be any kind of display generated by a computer's processor.

Neither the home TV nor the computer monitor can handle both types of signals without changing the nature of one of them. Either the digital output of the CPU must be transformed into an RF modulated waveform for display on the screen, or the video wave must be digitized for presentation on a computer monitor. Both methods are technically possible, but modulation of the computer's output is at present simpler and more effective than digitizing the video wave. Modulating the digital output of a computer produces fine imagery, as evidenced by numerous video games, home computers, and graphics systems.

103

But digitizing video information has two glaring draw-backs: first, it is so slow that it cannot produce a fast-scan image, and second, it produces a "mosaic" picture (Figure 2–18). By the same token, the standard television set simply does not provide the resolution or stability to make *extended* verbal communication through video transmission feasible. The break-up of character configurations and flickering of the type induce reader fatigue and annoyance. Further, the proportions of the oblong TV set screen are wrong for computerized displays.

Let's examine first the home TV features, quickly, and then the computer monitor's features at greater length.

The Home TV

RESOLUTION

The standard American 525-line picture is far too low a resolution for displaying characters and words that have to be read on an ongoing basis. Since the highest resolution count for *mass* market sets is 800 lines most manufacturers have focused their production and development facilities on this standard. Of course, others have not: Matsushita Electric (mother company to Panasonic and Quasar), as an example, is applying its titanic resources to developing many different methods for improving resolution and for making the mass market TV more compatible with nonbroadcast-reception applications.

The resolution problem is that the size of character cannot be so small that a slight breakdown in sharpness produces illegibility. To be read from the screen at a distance of roughly two feet, the characters of a CRT display must be slightly larger than the size of the type you are reading now. Hold this page at a distance of two feet (roughly arm's length, unless you are a gorilla), and you will understand the need. Now, because the type on this page is a solid black, it is perfectly "resolved"; that is, it is a clear and solid configuration. But characters on a data display are made up of points of light—of phosphor glow—in a matrix system. The matrix may be 5 × 7 (see Figure 3–6), 7 × 9, or perhaps larger. Some characters may be as large as a quarter-inch in height. The smaller matrix systems, however, 104 suffer most from this breakdown in resolution. Suppose, for

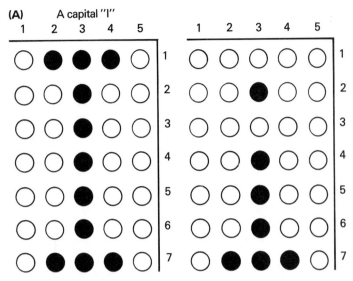

(A) A capital "I"

figure 3-6 A typical 5 × 7 matrix.

instance, the capital "I" in Figure 3–6 lost the two dots at the left and right of its base? Could it then be possibly read as a "T"? Matrix systems with a greater number of points grouped more closely together reduce the problem of illegibility due to poor resolution.

The 800-line tube, however, generally does not provide enough resolution for a sharp, clear character display. The slightest breakdown in transmission, reception, or processing causes letters—especially lower-case—to break up. For example, little "e's" become "c's," and "b's" look like "k's." The natural conclusion is to make the characters bigger, to improve readability and to overcome poor resolution. But this "solution" leads to two other problems: a waste of a lot of space on the screen and flickering.

WASTING SPACE

Naturally, larger characters cut into the number of characters and words that can fit onto the screen at a given time. With a standard sized character, a 12" rectangular CRT usually displays 32 characters in 8 lines for a total of 256 characters. That figure represents about as many words as are contained on a third of a double-spaced typed sheet of 8 1/2 × 11 paper. A 12-inch screen can also carry 16 32-character lines for a total of *105*

512 characters (32 × 16, or 32 characters/line × 16 lines). This configuration fits roughly two-thirds of a typed page onto the screen. To fit a full page, the same screen can also display 50 characters per line in 20 lines, yielding approximately 1,000 characters—or roughly the number of characters on a full 8 1/2 × 11 sheet. But now the characters are too small again, and we are back to the same problems with resolution. Another complication is that, if a screen is expected to present sophisticated color displays at a high resolution, then special graphic grids are necessary and are sometimes separate from the grid used for text editing.

Making the characters large enough to read easily naturally allows for fewer words on the screen at one time. The proportions of the home TV screen are about 4 to 3; another way of saying the same thing is that its "aspect" is 1.33 (4 ÷ 3). (See Figure 3–7.) In other words the screen is a rectangle resting on the long end. If it rested on the short end, it would be much more suitable for "page-like" data displays. However, the set— as is—can display a full "page" only at a small and troublesome

figure 3-7   The aspect problem.

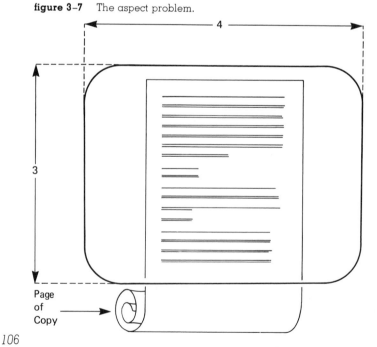

character size or only half a standard page at a readable character size (the aspect of half an 8 1/2 × 11 page is very close to 1.333). As a result, word processor CRTs have an aspect of 0.75, or 3 to 4, which is just about right for a page of display. Most general-purpose computer monitors are square and hence more "efficient" in their use of space.

STABILITY

Assuming we live with the larger characters, flickering also becomes a problem. The TV screen "refreshes" each phosphor dot 30 times a second. If the beam has more area to cover, it may not refresh the afterglow quickly enough for a perfectly stable image. So to ease the operator's eyestrain and to make sure the image does not flicker, terminal memories refresh the image approximately 60 times a second. Obviously, faster refresh circuitry works all the better. Any lower frequency can cause the imager to flicker and slowly wear on the user's eyes. Another method is to coat the screen with a phosphor that glows for a longer time. Many new anti-glare methods and coatings are being tried out these days.

To display a full page upright on a regular TV set, a resolution count of minimally 2,000 is necessary; 2,500 would be ideal. The type would still be small, but the character would be sharp and clear.

COMPUTERS THAT UTILIZE
HOME TVS

Despite the shortcomings, a number of personal computers utilize the home TV screen. In fact, one of the best-known makers of private computers, Apple Corporation, has worked wonders with the home TV set (Figure 3–8). For the general purposes of a personal computer these days, the TV does a fine job! But if users intend to build a sophisticated integrated system around the computer, the TV limits their applications. Whenever and if-ever standards are set for a universal teletext system that brings a printed page to the home monitor, the present TV specifications simply do not rise to IVT requirements (Figure 3–9).

figure 3-8   The Apple II, a leader in personal computers, is capable of producing color graphics on the standard 525-line TV set for its video output. Connected to a suitable color graphics terminal, it could serve as a low-cost, high-power personal video computer.

The Computer Monitor

Although basically a CRT, the surrounding circuitry in a true computer monitor differentiates it from the home TV. For one thing, it does not require RF-modulated input or an intermediate frequency to activate the screen. Another difference is that its manner of display may vary, depending on the intended application.

If CRTs vary, then which kind best suits the IVT application? In the long term, black-and-white screens certainly do not. Less certainly, but for good reason nonetheless, screens built into turnkey systems are not as desirable as separate monitors. Here's why.

BLACK-AND-WHITE DISPLAY

Although many fine color graphics monitors are on the market, most *non*personal systems utilize a black-and-white display. Of course, the phrase "black and white" is defined to include monochromatic (one-color) displays. Perhaps the reason for the preponderance of monochrome monitors is that they serve the majority of business applications well enough. In word-processing, data base utilization, accounting programs, and other standard business applications, a clear, sharp monochromatic image does very well. The same rationale holds true in educational situations. For both markets—large ones—manufacturers see no need to "overkill" the application with more expensive, full-scale color graphics software and hardware. Nor should they.

In this respect the market forces are conspicuously compelling the computer-making firms to cater to the virgin small businesses and limited educational systems. The fact that computers are becoming available to small institutional users constitutes "two steps forward"—toward the integrated video computer. The fact that the resultant products are limited in their display capability is only a small step back. Should graphic terminals become as popular and as versatile in home computers as the monochromes have over the past few years, then color graphics must eventually become a feature of institutional

figure 3–9   The Texas Instruments' TI 99/4 consists of a computer and separate color monitor. It offers up to 72K in total memory capacity, 16-color graphics capability, music and sound effects, an equation calculator, and a great deal of canned software.

Courtesy: Texas Instruments

systems before long. Its inevitability will eventually become a matter of what people *expect to see* when they turn on their computers.

Ineluctably, color must become standard. Color not only adds liveliness to displays, but it also pervades video presentations with easily discernible differentiations. A graph, for instance, is much clearer and vivacious if done in a number of colors. One color simply doesn't cut it.

BUSINESS COMPUTERS WITH BUILT-IN DISPLAYS

Plug-in-and-go (turnkey) consoles are handy, convenient, easy to use, and usually relatively inexpensive. In these respects, they serve many short- and long-term purposes. Their integration not only serves the needs of—again—nontechnical business and educational users, but it also constitutes a trend toward putting the pieces of a computer system together into a compatible whole. As a group, they constitute *de facto* recognition of the consumer's need for convenience and simplicity (see Figures 3–10 through 3–20.)

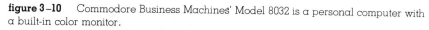

figure 3–10   Commodore Business Machines' Model 8032 is a personal computer with a built-in color monitor.

Courtesy: Commodore Business Machines

figure 3-11 (a) The Radio Shack TRS-80 is a complete low-cost microcomputer that is capable of handling a variety of clerical functions, with prerecorded cassette programs. With this basic model, Radio Shack was able to jump far ahead in the home computer market battles with Apple and PET.
(b) In 1980, Radio Shack announced the Model III, which includes among other features a 12" color monitor. Apparently, Radio Shack sees the oncoming need for color.

Courtesy: Radio Shack

figure 3-12   Compucorp's 625 Mark III is an integrated desk-top computer system, whose maker offers a wide line of software and hardware options. It is an excellent candidate for many business, educational, and other uses.

figure 3-13   The Durango F-85 is a portable microcomputer that puts a dual diskette, high-speed printer, central processor, keyboard with auxiliary 10-key numeric pad, and a monochromatic CRT—all on a desktop.

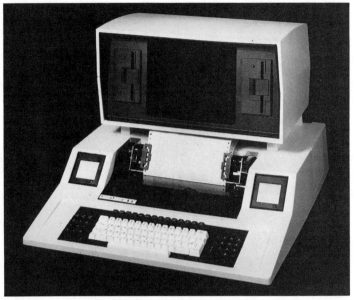

figure 3–14   The Athena Dt/C 8200 may be either a terminal or desk-top computer system. Its video controller module allows a 2-page buffer space, one on the screen and one "waiting." A 25 × 80-character format displays 160 various characters on a 9 × 12 dot matrix. White phosphor is standard, and green is an option.

figure 3–15   The Lear-Siegler ADM-31 is a greatly improved version of the firm's ADM-1A: a low-cost, high-reliability desk-top monochromatic CRT terminal that features a full 2-page display as standard equipment. It comes equipped with keyboard, control logic, character generator, refresh memory, and interfaces.

Courtesy:
Ohio Scientific

figure 3–16   The Challenger 3 Word Processing System is a high-powered business-oriented system with a monochromatic display.

figure 3–17   The Basic Four System 200 consists of a central processing unit, a 32K memory, a video display terminal, a 10-megabyte disc, a single-track 2.5-megabyte cartridge tape drive, and a 120-character-per-second bidirectional printer. The combined hardware/software system sells for $29,000.

Courtesy:
Basic/Four
Corporation

Courtesy:
Digital Equipment
Corporation

figure 3–18 The DEC station 78150 incorporates an LSI version of DEC's PDP-8 processor built into a video terminal. It employs a dual-density floppy disk drive with a 512K-byte capacity per disk. The VT100 video terminal, a PDP-8/A processor, and either RL01 (5.2 megabytes) hard disks, RX02 floppy disks, or a combination of the two—are all additional features.

figure 3–19 Even IBM limits itself to black-and-white display in its small business Model 5100 portable computer. Very versatile and user-oriented, it represents IBM's first serious bid for a part of the small business market.

Courtesy: IBM

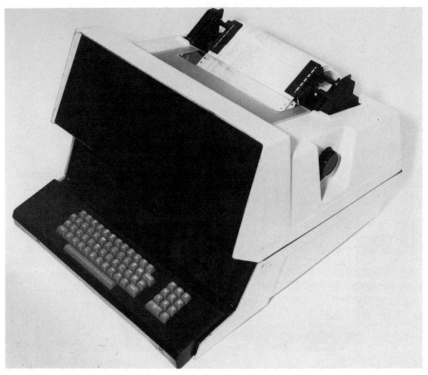

figure 3–20   The MVT/X3, built around DEC's LSI-II, is a powerful desk-top model compatible with many other systems: IBM 5100, HP8900, TI770, or any other desk-top system.

About the only disadvantage is that they restrict future expansion. If you are sure that the computer bought today will fill your needs tomorrow, then the system is for you. But if your long-term requirements call for the eventual use of a full-scale video computer system, then a turnkey obliges you to consider trading in or trading up for a whole new system. This future decision may or may not be a problem, but it certainly is a consideration.

WHAT'S LEFT?

Just from the point of view of display—and from that viewpoint only—the ideal computer monitor for use in an integrated video/computer system should have full-color graphics capability. Further, the monitor should be a separate module for possible future trade-ins or trade-ups. Such a monitor allows the user immediate flexibility in dynamic data displays and long-term benefits in keeping up with the improvements in the hardware. In June of 1979 Texas Instruments seemed to agree publicly with this conclusion by introducing the TI-99/4. Packaged in a separate keyboard unit, the 16-bit processor is interfaced with a separate color video monitor that is styled to resemble a TV set. (Do you wonder why?) The clear and sharp 13″ screen displays 16 colors on a 192 × 256 dot matrix in graphics mode; in the alpha mode, it offers 24 × 32 characters, also in color, in an 8 × 8 character matrix. Color graphics support is built into Basic, by which users can define their own characters.

THE BENEFITS OF
THE COLOR GRAPHICS
MONITOR

After establishing that a separate color graphics monitor is the best pick for an integrated system, the next logical question is whether it is a better pick than a regular TV set. A look at the market inclines many observers to say, "Yes, it is."

Many fine color terminals are on the market, and more are on the way (Figures 3–21 through 3–28). They are visible in every corner of the computer market, from the home computer to the million-dollar corporate baby. To take just one as an example, the "Renaissance Machine" (Compucolor II, Figure 3–21) is a home computer that, as of early 1979, was oriented primarily to individual entertainment through game playing. As such, it represents still another step in the progress toward the integration of color video and computer capabilities.

On the business front, color graphic terminals are becoming more feasible as the prices of microelectronic components drop. The greater number of applications for terminals and displays is process control and time-sharing services. The major obstacle to color terminals in the past has been cost. Now that this factor has been reduced drastically, owing to various technological innovations in solid state and circuit design, the black-and-white terminal and display market should be open to color ones. Public information displays constitute another area where color terminals will play a dominant role, particularly at airports.

figure 3-21   The Compucolor II has its own 8-color, 13" diagonal display (no TV interface). Characters are displayed in 64 × 32 and graphics in 128 × 128, including vector-generating software. The usable screen area is 10" wide and 7" high. A typewriter-like keyboard with color and cursor clusters, 27K of RAM and ROM memory expandable to 64K, an 8080 CPU, 7 baud rates from 110 to 9.6K, and a built-in mini-disc drive mass storage device are also featured. The basic terminal costs about $1,500.

figure 3-22   The Intecolor 8001G is a low-priced color graphics terminal used in a number of large-company computer applications. Its 13" diagonal, high-resolution CRT has a refresh rate of 60 cycles per second, an 80 × 48-character format (4:3 aspect), 128 characters in a 5 × 7 matrix (or a 6 × 8 dot matrix), 8 foreground and 8 background colors, and graphic plotting on a 160 (horizontal) × 192 (vertical) grid area. Software is available for vectors, bar graphs, and point plotting, as well as a "twice-up" character blow-up.

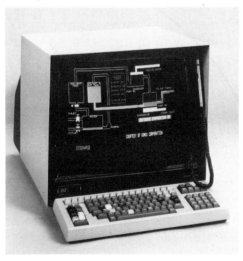

Courtesy:
Intelligent Systems
Corporation

figure 3-23   The Intecolor 8070 and 8071 are both parts of the Intecolor Series I business systems line. Both systems come equipped with the features of the 8001G, but they also have a 110-cps bidirectional impact printer for hard copies and an external dual 8″ floppy disc drive. The 8070 has 19″ color CRT, while the 8071 has a 13″ color CRT, with an additional built-in 5¼″ mini-floppy disc drive. The system also comes equipped with 16K of RAM and 17K of ROM. The screen uses 8K of RAM for refresh and the other 8K of RAM for workspace. The memory is expandable to 24K of RAM workspace and 15K bytes of special EPROM software.

figure 3-24   The Intecolor 8031 is a complete desk-top color microcomputer system with a 13″ screen and built-in single mini-disc drive with 80K bytes of storage capacity. Built around the 8080A CPU, the 8031 contains Disc Basic 8001 language which includes file-handling capabilities, a complete graphics package with graphics plot hardware, and expanded graphics software. The 8031 comes equipped with 27K memory, expandable to 64K. 16K of RAM is included, with all system software in ROM.

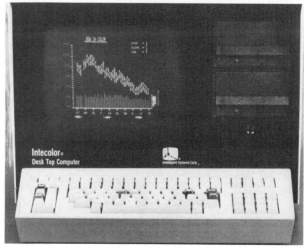

Courtesy:
Intelligent Systems Corporation

figure 3–25   The Intecolor 8051 is equipped with an 8080A microprocessor, a 19″ color CRT, and the standard ISC graphic features. For memory, the 8051 comes equipped with 21K bytes of EPROM/PROM, in which resides the Disc Basic 8001. The 8051 also incorporates 16K RAM, 8K of which is used for refresh, and the other 8K for user workspace. There is room for 16K bytes of additional user workspace. Total memory is expandable to 64K bytes. Storage is provided with an external single mini-disc drive with 80K bytes of data storage.

figure 3–26   The Hewlett-Packard System 45, with optional graphics software and four built-in interface ports, features a graphics mode of 560 × 455 matrix with a high visual resolution. Graphic CRT images may also be reproduced in hard copy form on an optional built-in thermal printer.

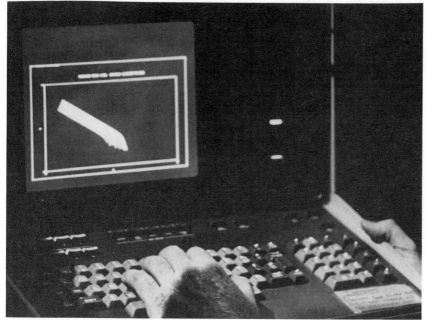

Courtesy:
Integrated Software
Systems
Corporation

figure 3–27   (a) ISSC produces extremely high-quality graphic output on both the CRT and plotter. The program is called DISSPLA®. Here an instructor demonstrates how to generate a plot on the CRT. Some of the undoctored results from the plotter are also shown.

(b) Because it is a multichannel system, Anagraph can be configured in a variety of ways to satisfy many an application. It can be a multiterminal system, driving up to sixteen fully independent display terminals. Or it can be a color display system with separate channels used to drive the different color "guns" on a standard color TV monitor. Channels can also be combined for form overlay or protected data applications.

Courtesy: Data Disc, Inc.

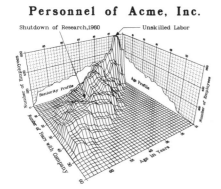

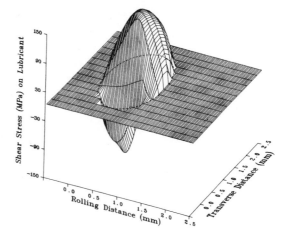

Courtesy:
Chromatics, Inc.

figure 3–28 Chromatics' low-cost, high-resolution color graphic computers and peripherals start at about $6,000. The line includes 13″, 15″, and 19″ color screen sizes with Z-80 full memory and I/O structure in a choice of 512 × 256 and 512 × 512 resolution. Other features are: full 8-color variable-size graphic and alphanumeric character options, keyboard-accessible graphic design with vector, circle, arc, rectangle, create, and overlay modes, as well as individual dot addressability.

1. *Production scheduling:* color coding of teams or departments, automatic reassignments due to changes in priorities, and so on.
2. *Financial and economic trend graphs:* demographic surveys presented on maps, multi-color and dynamic graphs for market action, among many others.
3. *Accounting applications:* color coding of receivable, overdues, to-be-billed, or payable accounts; color financial statements; and many more.
4. *Process controller:* the tracking of specific batches of orders through production; monitoring temperatures in energy-generating plants for safety; or almost any situation in which a change in color aids visualization or calls attention to important elements of the display.
5. *Marketing:* the sectoring of market shares by color designation in "what-if" models or the presentation of market survey results.
6. *Management Information Systems:* high-level management reports become more than words on a screen. They become a picture, which is more easily grasped and recalled. If the manager desires, he or she can access—quickly and easily—as

much up-to-date detail as needed to take action. While many current MIS systems now offer this ability, color video computers offer more ease of use than ever.

While this list presents only some of the applications of color graphics in business, the possible uses in medicine, education, government, the military, the arts, in the home and elsewhere are obvious. The business market, however, is the one with the need and the buying power. As color graphics prove their worth in more and more business applications, they will undoubtedly influence other markets to follow suit.

Graphics Display

THE GRAPHICS GRID

Computer CRTs solve most of the problems with displaying video/computer output but not others. For example, assuming that video information from a video recorder or camera can be displayed on the computer's CRT, should it dictate the aspect of the screen? All of ISC's specialized graphics screens are of the same dimensions as the home TV set: 4 to 3, or 1.333. That aspect makes its use in word processing systems difficult, unless expansive scrolling software and buffer storage are available. (ISC makes such features available in their more sophisticated models.) Apparently, the 4-to-3 ratio will endure, compensated for by manipulatory programming.

Despite this relatively minor drawback, the graphics grid networks of most specialized computer terminals make data display easy and at times startling and striking. The grid system consists of a cross matrix of RGB-phosphors groupings, each of which is easily accessed by the computer. For example, the ISC 512 × 512 graphics grid consists of 512 phosphor groups horizontally and 512 vertically. This cross-matrix therefore consists of over a quarter-million such groups (262,144 = 512 × 512). On their 19″ (diagonal) screen, the vertical dimension is approximately 11.4″ and horizontal about 15.2″. Given these dimensions, a phosphor group is located every 0.02227″ along the horizontal dimension and every 0.02969″ along the vertical side. To go one step further, each square inch on the screen contains roughly 34 rows of dots and 45 columns. All this arithmetic comes down to the fact that a square inch on a 19" (diagonal) 512 × 512 color graphics grid contains approximately 1,530 dots (34 × 45)—a fine basis for high-resolution color graphics. The effect of having more dots per square inch is demonstrated in Figure 3–29.

figure 3–29 The character on the left is composed of many dots in a fine cross-matrix. Hold the book at arm's length, and the letter seems fairly solid. Also at arm's length, the character on the right still seems fragmented because of the coarse nature of the cross matrix.

Colors are selected through the manipulation of these dots. Through complex and highly integrated circuitry, the depression of a color key signals the computer to illuminate all, say, green dots in any RGB group that is not otherwise activated according to a given program. Green is therefore the "background" color. Other background colors may be selected by mixing relative intensities of each color in an RGB group. Besides green, perhaps pink might be selected by raising the luminance (or light) content of the red elements, thus making them paler. Foreground colors may be selected similarly, but the location of each color must be pinpointed on the screen. The foreground colors represent the actual display elements.

The colors and their positions are selected in several ways. In video games, the excitation of the RGB groups in home screens is controlled by a canned program in the cassette or cartridge. On personal or nonpersonal computers—large and small—the color control comes from the keyboard, sometimes through isolated groups of keys or "clusters." Sometimes color can be controlled through light pens of "X-Y tablets" (Figure

3–28). Either of these two devices simply "reads" the position of the point on the cross-matrix and communicates that coordinate to the computer. While the light pen is touched directly to the screen, the scribe on an X-4 tablet touches the tablet instead. The tablet is only an electronic "duplicate" of the screen's cross-matrix; this duplicate feeds the scribe's movements across the face of the tablet to the CPU. The CPU accepts the data as if it were information from a light pen.

LIMITING FACTORS

Since all the factors affecting the quality of a CRT display are interrelated, they are difficult to discuss one by one. Any attempt to do so oversimplifies their mutual effects. Yet, four factors can be at least listed:

1. the numbers of points in a cross-matrix,
2. the size of the screen,
3. the speed of the CPU, and
4. the size of secondary storage.

Cross-Matrix Versus Screen Size. Suffice it to say that more points in the cross-matrix, faster CPUs, and larger memories all enhance not only the resolution but also the versatility of the display. More points per square inch allow the overall image to be finer in its quality. A 512 × 512 matrix produces a "finer" quality character on a 13" screen than it does on a 19" screen, because the RGB points are closer together on the smaller screen.

Table 3–1 shows how dense the points become as the screen becomes smaller with the same cross matrix. Such a table, of course, has practical limitations: 25" is about the largest a home TV can go right now, although some sets go as low as only a couple of inches. However, how much line resolution can be compacted into such small screens is necessarily limited (Figure 3–30). Notice in the table that a reduction in diagonal screen size of roughly two-thirds increases the number of dots approximately ten times.

Don't get the impression, however, that screen size and matrix limitations are so strict that they cannot be stretched by "pushing" the technology. For example, Tektronix, Inc., puts out   *125*

Table 3–1.   Comparison of a 512 × 512 cross-matrix on different-sized screens*

Screen Size (Inches)	Vertical Columns per Inch*	Horizontal Columns per Inch*	Number of Intersects on Screen	Number of Intersections per Square Inch
19"	45	34	262,144	1,530
13"	49	66	262,144	3,234
6"	142	106	262,144	15,052

*Assuming *all* the screen is usable; that is, no part of the screen is inaccessible by the actuating beam. All calculations are approximations simply for the sake of demonstrating a point.

**All calculations rounded to nearest whole number.

figure 3–30   Allegedly the first pocket television in the world, the Sinclair Microvision has a 2" diagonal screen, and it measures 4" × 6" × 1½"—about the size of a paperback book. It produces a sharp black-and-white picture which, when viewed at a distance of 1', is equivalent in its size and brilliance to compact models at 12'.

Courtesy:
Sinclair Radionics

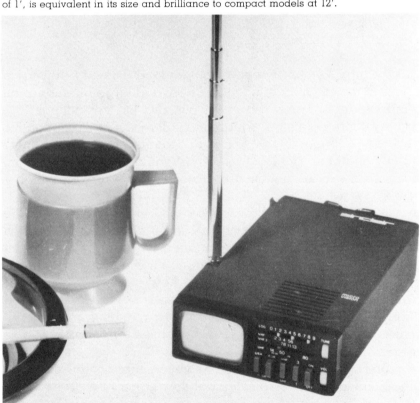

its Model 4027 Color Graphics Terminal that provides a 64-color palette, with up to 8 colors on the 13″ screen at the same time. The user may specify hue, luminance, and saturation by programming. That display is 32 × 80 with a large 7 × 9 character on an 8 × 12 matrix. Perhaps even more striking is the Model 384 by Systems Research Laboratories, Inc. This 25″ CRT operates at up to 34 kHz on its horizontal scan for a 1,024 × 1,024 pixel display. These and other "edge-of-the-industry" models, although high-priced right now, will likely become the CRTs of future video/computer systems.

To improve resolution on the existing, lower-priced systems, the question arises, then, "Why not simply include more points in the cross-matrices for larger screens?"

CPU Speed and Memory Size. The answer to that question has to do with the third and fourth factors in the list. Each dot has to be reactivated, you will recall, before the after-glow dies out. If the refresh cannot refresh the screen fast enough, the image flickers. Therefore, given its speed, the CPU can refresh only so many points sixty times a second. Faster CPUs can handle larger matrices. Although even the smallest and slowest of microprocessors can handle graphics displays of one sort or another, graphic sophistication is snipped off at the higher end by CPUs that do not work quickly enough to refresh large matrices.

A direct correlation exists, therefore, between the CPU rate and the size of the graphics display. On the low end, even such a relatively small system as the RCA Cosmac VIP has a color board module that permits the computer to display data in 3 background and 4 foreground colors. The former Cosmac could display only in black and white or on the home TV through a modulator. However, the Cosmac CPU does not permit a very complicated display.

Table 3–2 illustrates a number of points to remember: Notice in that table how the resolution increases from left to right as the CPU rate and memory size increase. Although the three right-most models all list "110 to 9,600 baud," within the product lines of each manufacturer, the graphics capability becomes greater as the baud gets faster. Screen size, within the range of 9″ to 19″, seems to be unaffected. And the number

Table 3–2. A sampling of color graphics terminals, cross-referencing CPU speed and storage to graphic capability

	Cosmac VIP	Compucolor (Model II)	Intecolor 8051
(Processor)	(RCA 1802)	(8080)	(8080A)
Speed	(NA)	110- 9600 band	110 to 9,600 band
Memory	2K RAM	27K of RAM & RAM expandable to 64K	21K EPROM/MROM 8K refresh 8K workspace Expandable to 16K workspace
Graphic Cross Matrix	8 × 8 (64)	128 × 128 (16,384)	160 × 192 (30,720)
Text Display	32 × 64 (2,048)	62 × 16 or 32 992 or 1,984	48 × 80 (2 × character mode 3,840)
Screen Size Diagonal	9", 12", 17"	13"	19"
Numbers of Background Colors	3	8	8
Foreground	4		

of available colors is almost exactly the same for all models, large and small.

Perhaps more significant is cross-matrix. Table 3–2 clearly demonstrates that the resolution of the display improves immensely as the main memory increases in size. The reason for this correlation is not hard to understand. Larger memories can store more complicated graphics programs, data, and operating systems. Although secondary storage can do the same, it cannot be accessed as fast as main memory. The lesson is that graphics display is enhanced either by the addition of main memory or by the utilization of virtual memory. Whichever is used, it must be fast enough to keep up with the refresh requirements of the screen.

IVTs
In the Making

Who's coming up with the ideas on integration? Apparently, the smaller you are, the more opportunity you have to move quickly with the times. Hobbyists and other individuals are

Courtesy:
Sharp Electronics
Corporation

figure 3–31 In Sharp's super-thin screen television set, the regular picture tube is replaced by an electroluminescent (EL) panel that is only 2" thick. The black-and-white set features a 6" diagonal screen and weighs just over 8 pounds. Although the set is not color and is not available in the United States as of 1980, it is an indication that the CRT tube is not the only way to display a video image.

extremely well suited for idle tinkering with the what-if propositions, even though their resources for development are clearly limited. At the other end of the extreme, the big sisters of Computerdom—IBM, NCR, Burroughs, Univac, Honeywell—are just as clearly limited in their flexibility. Besides the slow reaction time that comes with bigness, large corporations are in a sense "saddled" with their old million-dollar systems already in the field. A large portion of their resources has to go toward servicing these existing accounts. And on a public relations level, they cannot just turn around to longstanding customers and say, in effect, "Well all that equipment and software we sold you is no longer necessary!"

In between the two extremes are a number of medium-sized firms that have greater resources than uncapitalized individual hobbyists, but that have a lot of their "resourcefulness." Apple is a good example in the personal computer market—a company that grew from a garage operation to a

Courtesy: Cromemco **figure 3–32** The Cromemco System Three disc computer is an example of the typical small- to medium-sized business computer: Z80A microprocessor, 32-kilobyte RAM, dual disc drive, automatic progress execution when power is on, a fast line printer, and multi-user Basic. It has all that a business computer should have, and the company stands ready to tailor systems to fit specific needs. Perhaps most important, Cromemco rates extremely high on service and reliability, thus overcoming one of the biggest fears of first-time computer users—breakdowns.

multimillion-dollar enterprise in under five years. In the business world, Q1 corporation is such an organization. This small firm offers a fully portable (you carry it with one hand by the handle) and fully integrated desktop computer—the Basic Office Machine. Although it has no CRT, as such, it packs an efficient keyboard, bubble memory, six-line alpha display, modem capability, and high-quality line printer into a compact housing. Temporarily disregarding questions having to do with display, this sort of device reflects a high degree of break-through thinking (Figure 3–33).

The IVT, therefore, is not something that our grandchildren or even our children will luck into. It is a concept that is tipping on the verge of mass popularity—and computer makers in the know are rushing to meet that market with all they have.

figure 3–33   Q1's Basic Office Machine reflects the sort of integrative efforts that only young, flexible firms can incorporate into products. The BOM heralds the type of "hardware" we are likely to see more and more in offices all over the world.

In the home computer market, for example, Sharp is developing the Radio-computer, which, although not on the market as of the beginning of the eighties, will not be long in coming. (See Figure 3–34.) Comparing these two devices, you can easily see that the gaps between "home" and "office" computers are quickly closing. A computer is a computer!

Perhaps in recognition of these factors, some observers feel that IBM has to "break itself up" into a number of smaller companies. For example, in a speech at a meeting of the American Electronics Association in Costa Mesa, California in early November, 1979, Sid Webb, vice chairman of the TRW, Inc. and a nationally respected electronics expert, predicted that IBM would split up into four or five different companies during the 1980s, not as a result of government antitrust action but "because they want to." He stated, "IBM is a functionally structured company, and they're finding it's getting tremendously unwieldly." He noted the evidence for a potential split, their overlapping divisions, their unhappiness about the time it takes for them to introduce new products, and that they were seemingly on a hell-bent spree for modernizing and bringing things up-to-date. All this pointed toward their major split-up move at a rather early date.

Courtesy:
Sharp Electronics
Corporation

figure 3–34   The home computer of the future? This computer/entertainment center does it all. The keyboard not only contains the standard alphanumerics, but it also doubles as a calculator keyboard. It has a cassette deck for storage or for audio recording/playback. The screen can show you the latest game show or the results of a home-grown computer program. You can get VHF or UHF video, AM or FM radio, or the right time. And you can carry the whole thing by its handle. The technology is just around the corner.

Summary

The past two chapters have drawn close to several tentative conclusions:

1. Both domestic TVs and computer monitors have features that make them desirable in an integrated video/computer system, and both have undesirable features.
2. Black-and-white CRTs limit the versatility and dynamism of a video oriented system.
3. CRTs built into integral turnkey models present a possible compromise of capability in the future, should a better CRT hit the market.
4. The higher-quality CRT displays require a finer graphics matrix, a high-speed CPU, and larger main memory.

None of these conclusions answers the critical question with which the chapter started: Which is better suited to an IVT, the TV or the monitor? Unfortunately, that question still cannot be answered until certain other problems are solved. Particularly, is it easier to:

1. display data *and* video information in slow-scan on a computer monitor, thus making storage of both possible in the computer's external storage?
2. display both types of information on the TV, thus storing data in the computer's external storage and perhaps the "mixed" video on videotape (recorded from the TV)?
3. use dual screens, one for video and one for data, with a timer to coordinate both?

By investigating the nature of analog-to-digital and digital-to-analog conversion, along with the complexities of RF modulation, we should be able to decide on the most practical consideration.

chapter 4

A/D/D/A

Until recently, video and computer equipment developed along all but incompatible lines. Some of this incompatibility was undoubtedly due to manufacturers' helter-skelter efforts to service a ripening market, with only secondary regard for an enduring set of standards. If a manufacturer's primary concern was to set a standard, its underlying intention was no doubt to set the standard in such a way as to make all other manufacturers march to the beat of the one drum. Out of this furious bidding for market dominance is emerging more and more of an ackowledgement of the need for standardization. So this kind of incompatibility is rapidly being overcome with the cooperation within and between the industries, whose leaders now recognize the self-destructiveness of going off forever in all directions.

Other kinds of incompatibility, however, derive from the very nature of the equipment's function—specifically, whether it operates on an analog or digital basis. For a long time, video equipment produced only analog output, although the introduction of recent digital devices are making that statement less and less accurate. At the same time, home computers accept, process, and output only digital impulses. This inherent difference between the two types of output is a physical fact, not just a matter of specifications. One or the other, therefore, has to be modified for compatibility's sake.

Perhaps the best place to start, therefore, is with the configurations shown in Figure 4–1. Temporarily forgetting any optional peripherals and disregarding the need for a mixer and communications device, we can set up this configuration two ways, depending on the type of display screen selected:

1. the digital alternative, or
2. the analog alternative.

Basically, these systems illustrate a two-fold question: Should you alter computer output for compatibility with analog video and audio systems? Or should you digitize the video signals for uniformity with computer output? Either avenue is open right now to even personal computer owners, but the digital approach is still developing—extremely rapidly, but still developing. So those who adopt the digital configuration must understand that their systems must be extremely flexible thoughout the eighties at least.

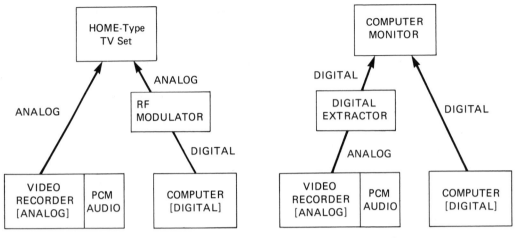

figure 4-1   (a) The analog system.   (b) The digital system.

Converting the World To Computerese

What specifically are the problems with digital extraction? The main problem is that sound and light exist in analog form. You have probably seen sound waves represented in their analog form on an oscilloscope: When someone speaks, the normally straight line jumps excitedly into peaks and valleys. In its analog form, sound can be recorded, but it requires too much processing time. The wave simply has too much data in it. Video signals have many times more, making the recording process even more of a hassle. Recording video for integration and display with computer output complicates the existing recoding problem—the need for analog-to-digital conversion. Similarly, although sound can be produced through a subsystem that is parallel to the video output components, recording and storing sound for synthesis and recognition are still practical only in digital form. Again, the conversion process is essential.

Digital means "segmented." You can take a length of an analog waveform and make any number of smaller segments of it (Figure 4-2, part 1b). Theoretically, therefore, an infinite number of "segments" exist between any two points in an analog wave form. So an arbitrary segment size is established.

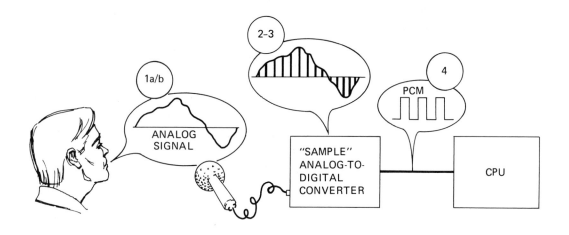

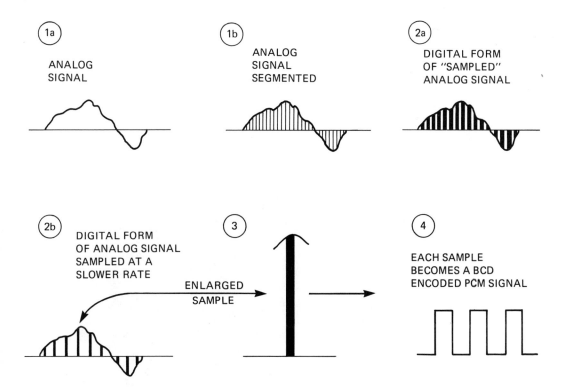

figure 4-2 An analog-to-digital (A/D) converter "samples" an analog signal and produces corresponding pulse codes for storage.

The analog–digital (A/D) converter (or extractor) divides the continuous sound into arbitrary segments and rounds them up or down to break up the wave into a series of electronic pulses (Figure 4–2, parts 2a and 2b). These pulses represent the analog wave in its digital form. In a computer system, the A/D converter is situated between the microphone or sensor, which feeds the analog wave to the converter, and the computer itself, which receives the digital form (Figure 4–2, parts 2–3). The digital pulse is the only form that can be stored in the computer's main memory.

The rate at which the analog wave is pulsed is called the *sampling rate*, and the resultant digital form is stored according to the computer's word size (Figure 4–2, part 4). The signal, as it is stored in the computer, is said to be *pulse code modulated* (PCM). A certain amount of *data reduction* (or *compression* as it is sometimes called) is necessary to compact any analog signal. Readings from sensor devices require the least. Sound requires more, and video the most.

figure 4–3   The Vector Graphic Precision Analog Interface Board enables an S-100 bus computer to input and output analog signals for a variety of measurement and control applications. The board contains two high-accuracy 12-bit digital-to-analog converters. Also operating as a successive-approximation analog-to-digital converter, it may input voltages from any of eight multiplexed analog input channels. A separate 8-bit digital output port is also on the board. All board functions are controlled by simple out and in commands, and D/A and A/D software is supplied on the board.

Courtesy:
Vector Graphics, Inc.

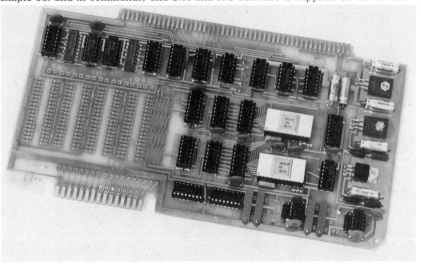

One of the many applications of computers of all sizes is environment monitoring and control. For example, you can enable a home computer to turn the houselights on and off for protection against burglaries. To do so, you might connect the computer to a light sensor as input and to an electromagnetic switch as output. As the sun goes down, the light sensor registers the diminishing light until it becomes little enough for the sensor to send an impulse to the computer. In turn, the computer goes into a timed program by which it sends impulses to several of the houselights, at irregular times, shutting them all off by, say, eleven in the evening. Sensing applications are obviously infinite in homes, factories, offices, schools, and almost anywhere. Range-scale systems involving hundreds of thousands—and even millions of dollars worth of equipment are in action all over the world.

Between the sensor and the processor, however, the analog signal has to be converted into digital form. And before the outgoing impulse can trigger a switch or other device, it must be converted back into analog form. These tasks fall to the A/D/D/A converters.

In microsystems, a number of these converters are available. For example, the Interfacer 2 is an I/O interface with 8 input and 8 output channels, controlled by Level II Basic. With it, TRS-80 users can connect the real world to their computers, in conjunction with switches, contacts, and other gadgets. Programs suggested in the accompanying manual are automatic telephone dialer, burglar/fire alarm, and a digital keyboard "combination lock."

The Pet Analog Input system digitizes signals from appropriate sensors for processing by Commodor Pet Computers (see Figure 4-4).

Generally, the amount of digital extraction required by such applications is small, compared to audio and video recording. Consequently, execution times are satisfactory.

SPEECH RECOGNITION

When you speak to a computer, you must speak into a microphone and through an A/D converter which translates your

figure 4–4 The System X-10 is a special-purpose computer that is custom-designed for monitoring and control operations in the home. It can operate lamps, stereo systems, TV sets, radios, fans, humidifiers, or anything electrical. And it is fully expandable.

spoken word into a digital "template." The average word can be stored in a 64-byte segment, which is the *template*. With some simple arithmetic, you can easily see that 64 such templates would require 4,096 bytes of storage, which is a 4K byte memory. Obviously, 64 words is not a large vocabulary, and a computer's conversational capabilities are limited severely and directly by its storage size. Part of the template is necessary for the address of the word. The word, stored in binary form is then addressed. The computer compares the templates in your voiced commands with templates in its storage by statistical methods. The closest match is accepted. If a match cannot be made within certain acceptable criteria, either the word is ignored or the computer asks for the word to be repeated. If the word has not been learned, the computer will never recognize the command.

Obviously, speech recognition systems are limited directly by the size of the memory. Actually, the ideal recognition system would be able to do what the human ear and brain do. The spoken English language consists of approximately forty variations in sound, each variation called a phoneme. If a program could be devised to recognize these phonemes, compare them with corresponding stored templates, and compile the templates for meaning, you could carry on a decent conversation with the computer. Perhaps the largest problem is with homonyms, such as "two" or "too" and "won" or "one" and "know" or "no." The human brain derives the correct meaning from the context: that is, it is capable of semantic analysis. Only some very sophisticated translation programs can do this now with up to 98 percent accuracy.

SpeechLab.™ SpeechLab is a typical speech-recognition system (Figure 4–5). If you know how this system works, others are pretty easy to figure out. Put out by Heuristics, Inc., the system includes the necessary hardware, manuals, programs, and high-fidelity microphone. It is compatible with any S-100 bus computer, such as Vector-Graphics, Parasitic Engineering, and Cromemco. Converter boards are available for many others. The circuitry consists of three audio bandpass filters, a zero-crossing detector, a compression amplifier, an A/D converter, a signal generator, reference calibration levels, and an analog multiplexer to interconnect the various functional blocks.

Here is how SpeechLab works: The assembled hardware is connected to the microcomputer system, and the software is loaded into the main memory of the computer. A program is then run that allows the user to "train" the system: Running the program actually creates the 64-byte templates that represent the utterances the computer is later to understand. Now the computer is ready (programmed) to learn how to hear and understand words. The user speaks a word into the microphone and types in on the terminal the code associated with that word. SpeechLab then digitizes the word into a 64-byte group and stores it in memory. Then, in a kind of random-access "read" operation, when the user speaks a word into the microphone, the board again produces a digitized version of the word. Only this time the computer compares the new pattern taught to the computer and chooses the closest match. Since everyone's speech waveform is unique, the computer might not recognize the word if it is spoken by anyone but the one who *141*

figure 4–5 The SpeechLab™ speech recognition system is compatible with any S-100 bus computers and correctly recognizes the spoken word 95 percent of the time. It consists mainly of a special circuit board and a microphone.

did the training. The manufacturers nonetheless claim a 95 percent accuracy when voices are "the same."

The recognition process is therefore two-level: The hardware receives the waveform and makes it automatically available to the software: then the software program compares the incoming data with the data in storage to make the match-up (Figure 4–6 is a flowchart of this process).

The reliability of the match-up depends largely on the sophistication of the machine. The SpeechLab manual contains graded experiments that allow the user to test the varying degrees of complexity. The system's software plots a graph on the screen for the user, so that that experimenter can visualize the data at different points in processing.

SpeechLab is educational, functionally useful, and as reported by many, a lot of fun. Anyone with a personal computer should be tempted to acquire a speech recognition system. Being able to command a computer by talking to it is definitely the way it should be—and the way it will be before very long.

Interstate Electronics Corporation.   The ultimate step is to program a computer to speak without having to actually train it with a human voice at all. This kind of computer talk is true speech synthesis—the kind of talking computers you see in science fiction movies. A step has been taken in this direction. Inexpensive systems, now available, actually synthesize English. Circuits that receive input in the form of a string of characters—each of which represents a phoneme—produce the analog signal needed to drive a speaker according to preprogrammed instructions.

Interstate Electronics Corporation has developed, for instance, the Voice Data Entry System, a sophisticated commercially oriented voice recognition/synthesis system that enables the user and machine to converse, with certain machine-training requirements (Figure 4–6). Basically, its flexibility lies in the 240-byte pattern that the system creates for each of the words entered—as opposed to 64-byte patterns in microcomputer systems. This industrial set-up has options for many interfaces, user terminals, and (most importantly) mass storage, which right now is the key to flexible realistic voice output. This is not a personal computer system, but it is indicative of things to come in microcomputers. It presents the question, "If the standard or minicomputer can do it, how long will it be before a micro can?"

In late 1979, Interstate answered its own question by introducing a 7 × 12″ single-board automatic voice recognition module that is multibus-compatible. With better than 99 percent accuracy, various models (for about $1,000 to $2,000) recognize 40, 70, or 100 words or short phrases in from 1 to 1.5 seconds. Each word undergoes spectral analysis, compression into a 128-byte signal, and digital processing. Although the system is presently speaker-dependent, the firm plans to produce speaker-independent systems before long. In so doing, Interstate placed its technology within reach of home computer enthusiasts.

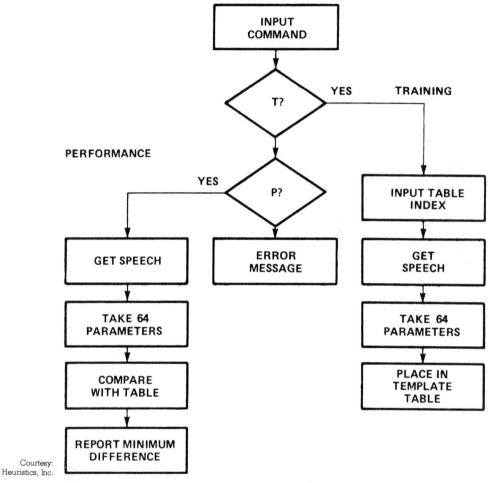

Courtesy:
Heuristics, Inc.

figure 4–6   The general flowchart for SpeechLab™ operation. The "T?" means, "Are we in the performance phase?"

Hitachi.   On a higher cost level, Hitachi designed the HR-150 speech recognition system. Its high price—$22,000 to $67,000— is justified by the fact that it recognizes voice commands regardless of who is speaking. It is not a "one-user" system. The HR-150, although too costly for home systems, represents capability that inevitably will be incorporated into microsystems
144   at low cost.

Speech synthesis is theoretically a lot easier than speech recognition. The PCM code is sent to the digital to analog converter, in which the codes generate voltages corresponding to the samples taken during the A/D process. These voltages then produce corresponding analog soundwaves through a conventional speaker (Figure 4–7).

figure 4–7   The digital-to-analog (D/A) process is essentially the reverse of the A/D process.

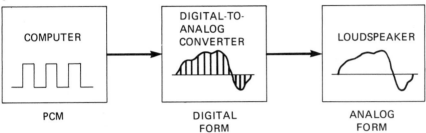

COMPUTER	DIGITAL-TO-ANALOG CONVERTER	LOUDSPEAKER
PCM	DIGITAL FORM	ANALOG FORM

The forty phonemes, stored in a moderately sized main memory, can be called out via programs in this manner in the proper sequence to form words. Each phoneme would consist of a predetermined set of PCM codes, and the sequence would depend on the program. But the user must program the computer's speech word for word: such programs would actually contain a list of phonemes that, when called out in sequence, resemble a statement in English. The program, of course, must contain a "Speak" command or its equivalent to send the phoneme to a circuit board which will actually produce the sound.

Practically speaking, this kind of computer talk is limited by the amount of main memory available, since each second of speech requires about 10K to 20K bytes. Lately, however, storage capacity has been used more efficiently because of data reduction techniques: These techniques eliminate some of the redundant digitized data from the analog sound wave. As a result, more "sound" is stored per K, but the sound is less like a human voice. In other words, you trade off speech clarity for   145 storage space and consequently a larger "vocabulary." The actual sounds are produced when the central processor sends the pulses connected with the programmed phonemes through synthesizing circuitry to a speaker.

This circuitry represents a remarkable breakthrough: Anyone can program a computer to talk without the individual saying a word. One drawback is that the speech produced by true synthesizers is not of the quality of the digital voice recorders, because the human rhythms and stresses are lacking. The speech is thus "robotic" and takes some getting used to.

Ai Cybernetic Systems.   Surprisingly, not all the devices with the true speech capability are most highly priced. In fact, they are quite reasonable. For example, Ai Cybernetic Systems Model 1000 Speech Synthesizer sells for under $400. The Model 1000 is a true speech synthesizer; it can say anything. It is a hard-wire version of the human vocal tract. Various circuits simulate the vocal cords, lungs, and mouth. Words and sentences are formed as strings of ASCII characters. Whereas a printer would cause a certain keystroke to produce a typed character, a speech synthesizer emits a certain sound particle, or phoneme. The phonemes (usually of standard Midwestern American English) are programmed into on-board ROMs. Any one phoneme is called out by supplying its equivalent ASCII character representation, as it is defined by the manufacturer. The speech rate and vocal pitch are adjustable for personal preference. The 12' output cable terminates in a standard miniature audio plug so the board can be patched into any speaker-amplified system.

Computalker.   Another true speech synthesizer is the Computalker by Computalker Consultants (Figure 4–8). The Computalker has more than true speech synthesis; it also is said to accept as input voice commands from cassette tape recordings. It is also compatible with any computer with an S-100 bus. Computalker is not only capable of standard digitized speech synthesis, which the average home computer memory can handle, but it also allows automatic data reduction for larger vocabularies.

Courtesy:
Computalker, Inc.

figure 4-8 The low-cost CT-1 Computalker board can synthesize human speech in any language or dialect, sing, and play music after being programmed by specifying the desired acoustic speech structure. Once the system has been "trained," the computer can speak.

The Computalker Consultants' CT-1A synthesis-by-rule voice module furnishes Apple II owners with 7,200-bps-produced speech. The device sells well below $600 and requires at least 16K of RAM (but 32K is better). All the required hardware and software is included except speaker and headphone. Owners of S-100-bus-based computers can obtain the same features with the CT-1, which is designed for the Radio Shack TRS-80 users, although Radio Shack markets a plug-in voice-response system for its TRS-80 microcomputer priced at below $400. This latter system produces not only voice, but special effects as well. It is made for Radio Shack by Votrax and constitutes a low-end addition to an impressive line of synthesis-by-rule voice-response systems.

Ohio Scientific. The "Home Computer of the Future" is the C8P DF model that includes a full keyboard, Basic language, video display of 2,048 characters, up to 16 colors, high resolution graphics, sound output, a D/A converter for voice and music, joystick interfaces and a large library of software for entertainment, education and personal finance. The unit uses two 8" floppy disks and has an AC control interface to inject control signals on the AC power lines of a home to control remotely   *147* placed switches and dimmers. The computer has the ability to turn lights on and off, interface with wireless home security systems involving smoke detectors, door contact switches, an automobile burglar alarm and auxiliary devices. The C8P DF can also notify the police or fire department with an optionally equipped voice I/O system including a Votrax module output generating English speech in case of fire, break-in or house tampering. Through an optional universal telephone interface system, the computer can dial any telephone number and also answer calls and communicate via DTMF signals or its voice output as well as conventional 300-baud model signals. The suggested starting retail price was less than $2,600. But Votrax suddenly drew many competitors for these OEM (original Equipment Manufacturers) customers.

Mountain Hardware. SuperTalker allows the Apple II computer to output high quality human speech through a loudspeaker under program control. It consists of a peripheral card that plugs into a peripheral slot on the Apple, a microphone, a loudspeaker, operating software, and two SuperTalker programs. Initially, spoken words are "read" into RAM through the system microphone. Speech data in RAM can then be manipulated like any other stored data.

Votrax. Perhaps one of the most interesting offers to home computer hobbyists is the Votrax Voice Synthesizer from a dozen small computer suppliers. The Votrax has, according to the manufacturer's advertisement, "an unlimited vocabulary" composed from sixty-four human sounds that are applicable to English, Latin, Spanish, Russian, Japanese, and Yiddish. Amazingly, a hundred average English words require only 1,200 bytes of storage. A demonstration tape costs only $5. Software is also inexpensive, only $10. Programs include talking BASIC, Latin, and Spanish. The device itself costs about $600.

Mecca. Mecca puts out the Alpha-I system, which is actually a mass storage system with a sophisticated 3K operating system that attaches to the top of your home computer. To the right of the keyboard is a speaker enclosure, the "mouth" of the synthesizer. The memory system is dual channel: that is, one channel contains the data and the other, the voice. Numbers, phrases, sentences, or entire speeches can be accessed quickly under computer control.

Cosmac. The RCA people have upgraded the capability of the Cosmac by putting out a $50 board for sound synthesis. Although not quite as sophisticated as other home computer boards, it is an indication that sound synthesis is no difficult task for even a simple computer.

Texas Instruments. Most recently, Texas Instruments has developed the Speak 'n Spell educational "toy" for children (Figure 4–9). The word "toy" is quoted for two reasons. First, it is essentially a spelling and vocabulary teaching instrument but an object of fun to children. Second, the technology that makes the vocabulary possible is extremely sophisticated for inclusion in a "toy." Actually, this toy represents a great advance in sound synthesis by computer circuitry.

Texas Instruments is a giant that can lead this sector of the industry and possibly dominate it. It was reportedly moving its low-cost ($90) speech synthesizer into small computers and into many other devices: learning aids, language translators, toys—

figure 4–9 (a) Texas Instruments "Speak 'n Spell" uses quizzes and games to teach children (ages 7 through 12) to spell and to pronounce more than 200 basic words. Using highly advanced integrated circuitry, it produces these words in standard American English.

(b) The Vowel Power™ module is the first in a series of plug-in word modules.

Courtesy: Texas Instruments, Inc.

and even its larger minicomputers. TI's TM990/306 is fully compatible with TM 990 microcomputer modules used in industrial control applications. Its constructed sentences replace the usual indicator lamps and alphanumeric displays. Although the basic vocabulary contains the numbers 0 to 12, the entire alphabet, and standard characters, it can be expanded considerably by combining certain letters and words. For example, the letter "N" can be prefixed to the word "crease" to pronounce "increase," while the letter "D" added to "crease" produces "decrease." Obviously other words, such as "be," "are," "you," "see," and "why" can be produced by using the appropriate letter. The total basic vocabulary is more than 160 words. The minicomputer's price at the opening of production quantities was from $1,280—and going down.

The Centigram MIKE voice recognition and response unit permits oral input and vocal response from an external computer. Supplied as stand-alone unit or as an individual board, MIKE recognizes 16 words and short phrases, responding with up to eight seconds of audio messages. Expansion options include 10 additional, 16-word vocabulary sets, and memory option doubles response capability. The price is in home computer and very small business system ranges: recognition-only electronics run for less than $1,800.

Telesensory Systems, Inc. Telesensory Systems, Inc. offers a programmable digital signal processor in two LSI chips. This particular processor vocalizes computer outputs in scores of telecommunications systems, particularly optical character readers, to produce an ASCII-formulated text. One of two microprocessor-based modules converts this character stream into phonemes at a rate of several thousand bytes a minute; the second (host) microprocessor then translates the phoneme string into a sequence of control parameters for the vocal tract model in use. The output goes to a digital-to-analog converter and then to a loudspeaker. The price? Under $200.

Other Companies. The Data-Bag™ speech processor by Mimic Electronics allows users to digitally record their voices in the computer's memory and then play them back by having the computer output those memory contents through the D/A section.

As of early 1980, over 20 companies were in the "computer voice" business. As 1981 opened, many more were coming. In late 1979 Voicetek, for example, launched its first entry into the voice input/voice response market. The system, COGNIVOX, plugs into the Exidy Sorcerer personal computer. It recognizes and can respond with 16 words or phrases. Software includes Voicetrap (a voice-operated video game) and Vothello (a vocal-input version of the game, Othello). Master Specialties, Inc. of Costa Mesa, CA. offers its Model 1750 voice-response system which operates from a ⊗12V power source. Mimic Electronics Co. offers delta-modulation techniques with its speech synthesizer system.

In mid-1979, Motorola Inc. advertised, "Digitize voice fast, not furious, with one $6.95 CVSD interface IC." The ad went on to say, "Now there's a quick, easy, flexible and very economical way of voice encoding/decoding: the single chip, MC3417/3418 CVSD, or continuously variable slope delta modulator/demodulator." ITT Semiconductors Group offers a digital speech generator circuit intended for use in consumer applications. It accommodates all the necessary speech elements for a vocabulary of more than 20 different words, together with the required control circuitry. Words are combined in any order to provide oral, step-by-step operating instructions.

So rapid are developments in recognition and synthesis that they show up in many types of electronic devices: color TVs, digital clocks, calculators, microwave ovens, timer units, cassette players, and soon. Toshiba, for instance, is experimenting with a typewriter that recognizes 100,000 to 200,000 Japanese words by identifying the language's 6 basic syllables. Toshiba also produces a voice-activated TV set and hifi set (Figure 4–10); Sanyo also offers a TV that responds to voice control. Its accuracy response is better than 90 percent. IBM produces a synthesis device that attaches to their mag card devices. The attachment scans typed copy and "reads" it back aloud to blind typists, thus eliminating the need for dependence on sighted co-workers.

NEC America, for example, announced its voice data entry system, the DP-100 that recognizes "fluid," connected speech for input into computers or control machines. That is, users may use their normal, everyday speaking rate. And Nippon Telegraph and Telephone Public Utility Co., for instance, reports *151*

figure 4–10   (a) Toshiba's voice sensor television set is controlled by the human voice. All the viewer has to do is to give a spoken command to turn the set on or off, choose or change channels, or adjust the volume level. The set says "Okay" when the command is accepted and "Repeat" when it is not understood.

(b) Toshiba is also working on a personal music system—an Acoustic Remote-Controlled hi-fi Component System (ARCS) that will respond only to the registered owner's voice. The voice control system can perform any of 19 different operations in response to the spoken word.

Courtesy: Toshiba America, Inc.

generating a speech synthesizer on a single chip. And a professor at Kyoto University is bringing about a voice recognition device that translates words spoken by anyone into printed or screen-displayed characters. While these achievements are temporarily out of the reach of the home computerist, they won't be for long. Keep your eye on the East!

These are only some of the many, many products out in the voice recognition and synthesis field. If you already own a home computer, or if you are considering a purchase, you might consider some of the advantages of an additional system that enables you to communicate more directly and naturally with your machine.

THE DIGITAL PROCESS IN AUDIO RECORDING

Previous sound reproduction worked entirely on the analog principle: Recorded signals were direct images of the actual but imprecisely transcribable musical waveforms. The analog process has the distinct weaknesses, like most analog techniques, of distortion and noise. As dozens of noise and distortion-suppressing devices, gadgets, and components have been invented and marketed to reduce these and other analog drawbacks, the history of hi-fi systems has been a continuous and expensive effort to improve the playback quality of the analog system without changing it. In the newest sound systems, therefore, analog techniques have been relegated a position of only secondary interest, and digital is "in."

Due to its pulse coded form, digital recording is referred to most commonly as pulse code modulation, or PCM. The sound is nothing more than the result of the number of pulses used to express each segment of the sound wave. The minute, precise original pulses actually spell out the wave form for a sound never before possible. So great are the results that most sound experts unanimously refer to PCU as a "revolution" in sound. *Radio Electronics* (February, 1978) called digital sound the biggest breakthrough since Edison first preserved his words on a tin-foil cylinder. In December 1977, the Japanese magazine, *JEI*, stated, "Just as 1877 will be remembered as the year Thomas Edison invented the phonograph, so will 1977 go down in the annals of audio as the year that PCM [Pulse Code *153*

Modulation] arrived . . . ." *Consumer Electronics*, in October of 1977, compares digital sound with " . . . the coming of electrical recording in 1926 and stereo in 1958." It is indeed a revolutionary development—no doubt about it!

The PCM revolution has seized upon the disc as its medium. Tape simply does not have the stability or density that a disc has. The means of recording is by laser only. Mechanical means are not accurate enough. In recording, the sound is first pulse code modulated and then frequency modulated. The resultant signal controls the beam that "cuts" the disc. In playback, the laser in the player "reads" the cuts, feeding a preamplifier, an FM demodulator, a dropout compensator, and finally a D/A converter. Hence the revolutionary sound.

The laser also offers other advantages, such as a practically infinite disc life, random access to specific sections in a split second, easy repeat playback, negligible wow and flutter, a range of as much as 98 decibels, a frequency response from 10 Hz to 20 kHz, no distortion or tracking error, no rumble from outside vibration, and no surface noise. How do you beat all that?

The recorders are becoming available, first to institutional and then to individual users. For example, Mitsubishi, TEAC,

figure 4–11 Sharp's talking calculator employs a voice synthesizing system that verbally confirms all calculating processes at each key operation, ensuring the user that each figure is entered correctly. The unit also offers a playback function to check calculating processes, a memory capacity of up to 100 steps with a step counter, three-position voice adjustment (fast, normal, slow), and twelve-digit, two-memory.

Courtesy:
Sharp Electronics Corporation

and the Tokyo Denka Company have jointly developed the audio PCM laser recorder. In recording the system converts audio signals into PCM signals, modulates them into FM digital signals, then records them by laser beam onto the disc. During playback, servos manipulate the laser optics system to read out the signals. A playing time of 30 minutes has been achieved by using a polyvinyl chloride disc. The companies expect to extend this time to two hours per disc.

In contrast to the disc system, Sony Corporation has marketed a PCM audio tape unit for professional use, the PCM-1600 (Figure 4–12). This requires a wide bandwidth (more than 1 mHz) in order to record the digital signal. The user needs a VTR with a high recording density to record the PCM signal containing two channels of audio information within the video band.

figure 4–12 The Sony professional PCM tape audio unit (left) and a professional Sony VTR.

Courtesy:
Sony Corporation

Sony maintains that you can use tape to record and play back the on/off signals of data storage for computer applications without error, then PCM recording can be accomplished as well on tape as on disc. This unit uses either 13 or 16 bytes for each channel of information. With a 16-byte linear quantification, the theoretical value of 85.5db is obtained for dynamic range.

This small and light weight unit requires no VTR modification. Its complete dropout error correction is based on special error-correcting codes. Wow and flutter are below measurable limits. Electronic editing is possible by using a video editor, digital-to-digital dubbing is possible, and synchronized operation is possible with VTRs and other PCM audio units. Furthermore, there is no quality deterioration on playback thanks to digital output error correction.

As the eighties opened, the names of manufacturers that have been involved in disc research all along continued their involvement. Many sought to make PCM audio players out of video tape equipment. Toshiba, for instance, offered a PCM adapter for Beta VCRs, as did Sony for both Beta and VHS players (for professional applications only).

Most of the by-now familiar firms, however, were exploring the PCM audio capabilities of discs. Again, Toshiba put out two PCM audio disc players. North American Philips offered its Compact (4.5") Disc that offered PCM sound through an optical picking unit. And AEG-Telefunken joined hands with Decca in a joint venture to sell PCM audio-disc systems. (Klaus Werner of Telefunken stated that such systems should eventually go for about $550 and that they will exist side-by-side with analog systems well into the 1990s.)

As always, the standardization issue raises its head. Standardize too soon during a formative phase in technology, and creativity is stifled. Standardize too late, and the mass market

figure 4-13 The PCM deck of this digital player/recorder monitors tape, just like analog-type decks. Editing can be conducted on this unit in much the same way as on conventional tape decks.

Courtesy: Mitsubishi

is missed because it becomes too involved in specifications. In June of 1979 a meeting of the Digital Audio Disk Council in Europe yielded the conclusion that PCM disc players should have a standard compatible with video disc systems. But video disc systems are split between two camps: mechanical systems are manufactured by Matsushita (Panasonic) and Japan Victor Corp.; optical systems by the others—Sony, Hitachi, Mitsubishi, Toshiba, Philips, Thomson. As a secondary finding, therefore, the Council realistically concluded that they might have to settle, at least temporarily, for a dual standard. In this spirit, Sony and Philips have agreed to exchange patent information fully—simply for the sake of greater compatibility.

THE DIGITAL PROCESS IN VIDEO RECORDING

As Passive Entertainment.   Video information can be stored on discs in PCM form, just like audio and computer data information. However, because fast-scan video output requires more information per unit of playing time, videodiscs have a shorter playing time than audio discs. Also, since computer data is far more "compact" than video information, a disc can contain many times less video content. Nonetheless, the disc still beats tape for sheer volume of storage. Again, the only drawback seems to be the read-only characteristic.

Combining the storage feature with its greater durability and greater accessing versatility, the disc presents quite a threat to videocassette sales. In reaction to this threat, just about every electronics firm in America and abroad is working on a videodisc player or has one on the market.

Unfortunately, despite the rush to stake claims on the entertainment market (Chapter 2) the videodisc player merely substitutes one form of passive entertainment (a prerecorded disc) for another (broadcast or cable programming). Given the titanic potential of the user-programmable or user-recordable disc, manufacturers would be insane not to allocate at least a portion of their R&D budgets for work on this problem. Drexler, for one, is working on a user-recordable video disc with prerecorded servo guide tracks.

It is also unthinkable that qualified individual enthusiasts are not slaving at a solution. An indication of the activity is the announcement by a Canadian inventor, John Locke, that he has developed an erasable videodisc system with a 5- to-10-milliwatt laser. He is supposedly negotiating with two companies for the developmental rights. Further, in mid 1977 Hitachi (a close collaborator with General Electric in the United States) developed a prototype of an optical videodisc laser recorder that can record 50,000 to 100,000 signatures on 30-cm videodisc. It can also retrieve and reproduce a frame in 0.5 to 3 seconds. The picture information is sent through a TV camera or VTR, and it is recorded by a laser beam 0.6 micron meter in diameter (1,800 rpm).

For Active Displays.   The furor over the use of the disc as a vehicle of entertainment sometimes obscures the applicability of the digital process in other areas of video recording, storage, and display. A video image—a live subject viewed through a camera or an electronic image received through an antenna—can be digitized for storage in a computer's memory. Further, that image can be reproduced on a display screen directly from the processor or communicated like any other type of computer data over phone lines or satellite. A typical configuration is shown in Figure 4–14. All the equipment represented in that diagram is on the market right now. Assuming a person owns a color television (which may be used) and a personal computer without a floppy disc, the cost of developing the system would be approximately $800.

Other Configurations.   A security application warrants the set-up shown in Figure 4–15a. If a human receiver is always present, then no computer is necessary at all. Just the converter is necessary to use the existing phone lines for transmission. No transmission is necessary. If it is, then add a VTR, as shown in Figure 4–15b. If no human observer is in charge of the security system, then a simple process—a control computer—may be added (Figure 4–15c) to trip off an alarm or a prerecorded message to the police or fire department. And if an unattended system requires not only response by the computer, but record-

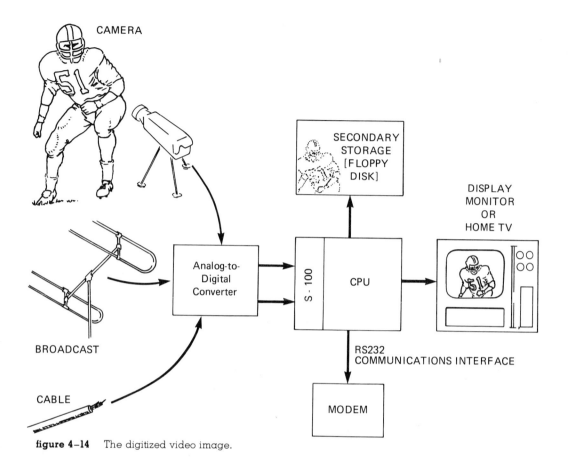

figure 4–14 The digitized video image.

ing as well, then a VTR and monitor can be attached to the layout so that the nature of the security problem can be recorded while the computer takes action (see Figure 4–15b). As you might suppose, this system need not be confined to security applications. The camera could be focused on a scientific subject, a production line, or any subject that requires video recording. Also, the A/D converter is necessary only when transmission of the image must take place over a distance, thereby necessitating the use of the phonelines medium. The equipment for A/D and D/A conversion is available, as is every other piece of equipment in Figures 4–14 and 4–15.

So why isn't A/D conversion used universally to convert fast-scan video images into data bits that can be easily transmitted, stored, and processed?

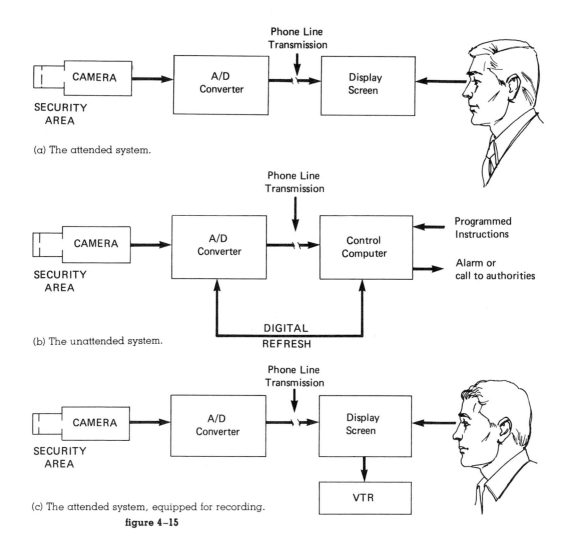

(a) The attended system.

(b) The unattended system.

(c) The attended system, equipped for recording.

figure 4–15

THE DISC AS SECONDARY STORAGE

Without doubt, the disc can store more computer data than most other media. Square inch for square inch, it is among the cheapest forms of storage. Tape storage cannot be compared because its density/cost ratio is so divergent from that of disc. The floppy or mini-floppy disc costs the user approximately $50 per megabyte, while disc storage ranges from a fraction of a cent to about half a dollar. Its storage capacity in general is amazing. Any information stored on a full capacity disc in binary form permits storage of 1.25 billion bytes per disc side, a total of 2.5 billion bytes per disc—all random access! While such capacity lends itself to highly interactive programming—especially in business or education—the read-only nature of the disc renders it a purely institutional medium. Home or personal computer users simply cannot afford to have their own discs "cut"—nor is there a need in the home market.

By 1980, several disc-oriented firms were getting into the storage potential of discs. North American Philips had a prototype that could store 20 million bytes on two sides, while the ever-present Hitachi was working on a disc that would store 10,000 to 20,000 facsimiles. In the meantime, the Mogiec Division of Magnavox was developing a 20-gigabyte, laser-scanned single-disc memory with an access time of only a half-second.

Perhaps of greater interest is the involvement of such big fish as IBM, Exxon, Xerox, or Atlantic-Richfield. IBM and MCA, Inc. have formed a joint venture called DiscoVision Associates, which is to produce an optical laser disc device. IBM has donated two patents plus cash; MCA, its expertise in disc recording and playback. The other companies mentioned are all selling a (nonconsumer) optical laser disc player/recorder.

Once the disc becomes user-programmable, it could be the ultimate medium if developments in bubble memory, charge-coupled devices, or some other medium do not overtake the maturation of the disc. Very likely, someone will produce the user-programmable disc. It is illogical to believe that any large company would not want to be the first on the market with an erasable disc. Surely every electronics manufacturer in the world has *some* allocation of R&D money for work on this problem. The Drexler Technology Corporation is a good example. It has developed the ROMP™ disc, capable of storing 900 megabytes. It's cost per megabyte is between 5 and 9 cents. The disc stores data photographically on one-micron data on the surface of a silver halide solution. The company has also developed a system that permits the instant detection of errors during recording, a problem that had proved troublesome in the past. This enhanced disc medium is also read-only—a feature that the company contends convincingly is an asset when the disc is used for operating systems or set applications program. Whatever its press releases say, the firm is likely to   *161* have the staff working on user-programmability. MCA Disco-Vision is another company that is reportedly working on a disc recorder comparable in size and cost to a photocopier. The programmable disc is a distinct possibility, at least for the institutional user, in the near future.

THE DIGITAL PROCESS
IN THE INTEGRATED VIDEO
COMPUTER SYSTEM

Essentially, that question is the same as asking, "Why isn't the simplified digital layout in Figure 4–1a acceptable?" In a sentence, the state-of-the-combined arts does not allow as much latitude as the analog system, for several reasons. First, A/D boards cannot sample video signals fast enough to produce a fast-scan picture. So most digitized video signals take several seconds to form, and the viewer sees a series of one-, two-, or several-second frames "wiping" the screen. Second, the storage required for fast-scan TV is so great that most main memories cannot handle the needs; secondary storage, usually in the form of mini-floppy diskettes, is therefore needed. Secondary storage, however, takes longer to access and thus only aggravates the speed problem. Third, the resultant picture just doesn't look normal; it has a "digitized" look (Figure 4–16). Fourth, without high-cost dedicated lines, the transmission of digitized

figure 4–16   These photos were taken from screens displaying digitized video information. Note how the pictures look as though they are made of mosaic.

Courtesy:
Vector Graphic, Inc.

video information over normal phone lines does not take place fast enough to produce a fast-scan picture. We will discuss this point further in the chapter on communications. In effect, digital conversion yields a slower, lower-quality image. Such a system might be adequate for only security, lab, or other similar applications, but it does not make for the ideal universal video/computer system.

The Need for Speedier Main Memories.   To make the image faster and better looking, the computer's readily accessible main memory must be enlarged by several magnitudes. Traditionally, instead of enlarging main memory, developers have relied on enhanced external storage devices—largely mechanical and comparatively slow equipment, subject to mechanical failures. The advent of the LSI-RAM as a main memory medium for many large computers and for all microprocessor-based systems generally increased internal memory system at low cost. LSI-RAMs are speedy at retrieval, and since they are solid-state devices, they have no moving parts. But they are volatile: no power, no memory. Most external storage devices, on the other hand, can be pulled off-line for nonvolatile storage.

Bubble Memories.   Bubble memories (Figure 4–17) represent one type system to fill the "gap" between mechanical memories and LSI-RAMs. Bubble memories are solid-state, and they therefore have no moving parts. They're also nonvolatile, retaining data as external devices must do if the power is interrupted or turned off. They store and retrieve data faster than mechanical disks, drums, and tape systems. Further, bubble memories store comparable amounts of data in a few cubic feet of system area, where mechanical memories require rooms full of equipment. They operate on a few watts of power, while many mechanical memory systems consume so much power that they require 220-volt lines.

The very nature of the bubble memory's structure and function makes it a natural candidate for video storage sometime in the future. Thin films of certain magnetic materials, such as a layer of magnetic garnet artifically grown on a nonmagnetic garnet substrate, contain amorphous "domains."   *163*

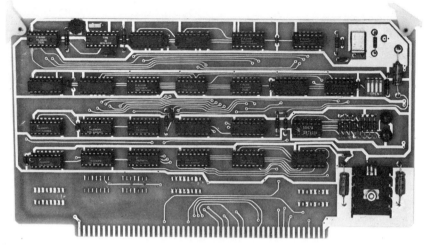

Courtesy:
Vector Graphic, Inc.

figure 4-17   The Vector Graphic Analog Interface Board is a multipurpose board designed to permit low-cost interfacing for any applications requiring digital inputs. A pair of pulse generators can be used to produce sounds for games or for keyboard audio feedback. The board occupies two input and output port addresses, which may be assigned anywhere from OO to FF hex. Analog conversion is accomplished by program loop testing a voltage comparator output and incrementing a register as a result of the comparison. A conversion with the resolution required for cursor motion takes about 480 μsec. The resolution of the A/D conversion is entirely under software control and can range from 16 or 64 counts for cursor motion to 1,024 or more for graph plotting or feedback controls.

(b) One-megabit linear bubble memory module for Rockwell's System 65, the R6500 microcomputer development system.

Courtesy:
Rockwell
International, Inc.

164

Courtesy: Rockwell International, Inc.

(c) Rockwell's 256K-bit bubble memory device (RBM256) photographed with a bubble memory chip on a magnified portion of the chip's circuitry.

When two permanent magnets, placed on either side of the film apply a magnetic bias field in a direction perpendicular to the film, these randomly shaped domains shrink into "bubbles" which are actually cylindrical magnetic domains of fixed volume whose polarization is opposite to that of the thin film. If the polarization of the thin film is south, then the bubbles are like floating islands of "north" in a sea of "south." These bubbles can actually be seen as contrast within the film when viewed under great magnification in polarized light. The bubbles enable the medium to "move" at extremely high speeds. Stable over a wide range of conditions, magnetic bubbles do not actually "move." Matter itself does not move. Rather the magnetic properties of the crystalline elements of the garnet are transferred extremely rapidly. To guide the control of this "movement," a permalloy pattern of chevrons is applied to the surface of the film to form "paths." When, in addition to the bias magnetic field, a rotating magnetic drive field in the same plane as that of the film is also applied by two coils which are part of the magnetic bubble device, the bubbles can transfer data extremely rapidly along the permalloy paths. The permalloy paths are formed as loops. A bubble in a certain position on the loop corresponds to a 1-bit; its absence represents a 0-bit. A *block* consists of bubbles in the same relative position in each loop.

Input and output in bubble memory is also less mechanical   *165* and thus speedier. Data is entered by generators at one end of the chip. Bit information is transferred in at gates, thus forming bubbles at known positions in the loops. In a read-out, the output circuitry includes a detector that transforms the bubble into an electronic pulse. This "read" operation preserves the bubbles as they are on the device, making nondestructive readout a prominent feature of bubble memories. A different kind of output can be used to transfer (or "erase") the bubbles.

Bubble memory technology, in short, is expected to create as big a revolution in computer memories as the microprocessor has in a large number of products. Many future applications for both bubble memories and microprocessors have yet to be imagined, and presumably at least one will be in the storage and speedy accessing of digitized video information.

In 1978 Rockwell, Texas Instruments, Intel, and Fujitsu began a race to the market with a bubble device. In late 1979 Intel announced a new "commerically available" device able to store a million bits of data on a single chip, the 7110. This megabit device complemented the smaller capacity Rockwell bubble memory M256, and the two are the "workhorses" of Rockwell's bubble memory business through the mid-eighties offering speed and capacity options. Looking further into the future, new fabrication techniques now being developed by Rockwell's scientists promise bubble memory devices able to store at first four million and later up to 16 million bits on a chip about a centimeter square by the mid-eighties. These devices will be produced by surely many manufacturers with technologies that will also enable the fabrication of fantastically more dense microprocessor devices.

The Converter in the IVT. Should bubble memory—or some other similar innovation—so enhance a computer's main memory at low cost, then one of its applications must necessarily be a high-speed analog-to-digital interface board. Such a device, if fast enough, could provide the speed *and* capacity for fast-scan, high resolution digital displays. Bubble memory's role would be, partially, as an automatic A/D converter within the CPU (Figure 4–18). The expanded version of this configuration is shown in Figure 4–19. However, Rockwell's first "sample" bubble memory board in late 1978 cost $500, and prices will probably not be at the home computer market level—the mass

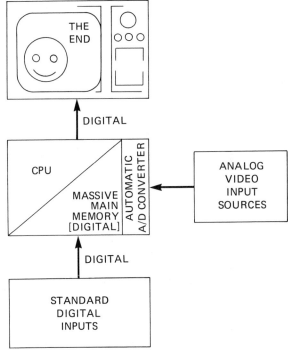

figure 4-18   The video system with an ideal main memory system.

market applications—until the mid-eighties. So the likelihood of sufficient main memory to accommodate such a configuration as that shown in Figure 4–19 is not great for some years to come.

Another possible application, however, may make the bubble memory board part of the IVT sooner. If a bubble device, with sufficient speed, were to be utilized as an A/D converter, it could prove to be the high-speed digital extracter needed for Figure 4–20. The expanded version of that configuration is shown in Figure 4–21. The only difference between this layout and that in Figure 4–19 is that the A/D conversion takes place *outside* the CPU, thus allowing the process more "working room" for operating and applications programs. The latter configuration also permits VTR and computer owners to complete the integrated system simply by buying an interface board. The system in Figure 4–19 would require a revamp of an existing computer system, perhaps a whole new system. It would also render the video recorder an optional peripheral.   *167*

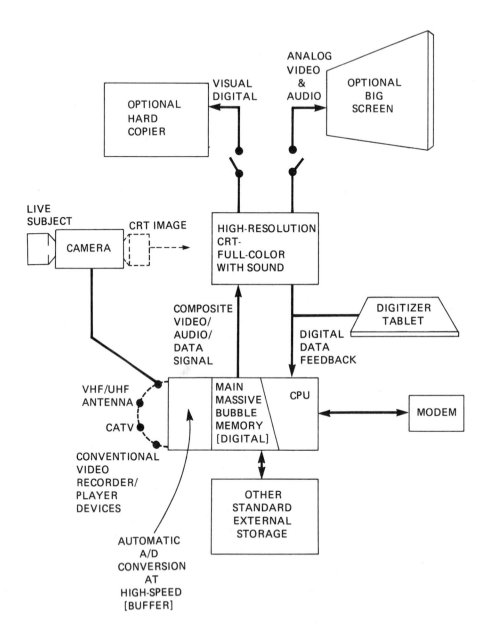

figure 4–19   The expanded version of the bubble memory digital system.

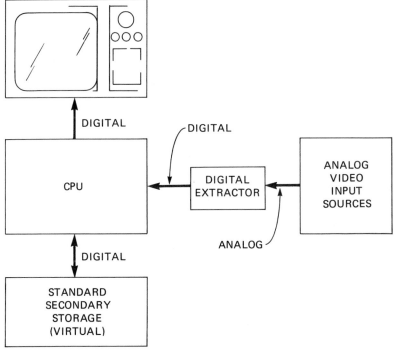

figure 4–20 An alternate digital video/computer system.

Note therefore the following characteristics of both systems:

1. The video recorder can input video signals, along with any other video device. It is no longer an essential part of the system.
2. No SEG device is necessary to mix video and data information, because all graphic control is under the control of the CPU's program or the user's keyboard.
3. Neither is an editor VTR necessary to edit tapes or discs, since all control of the display is under the guidance of a program and recorded via the camera.
4. To take a dynamic "hard copy" of the composite graphic display, the camera would have to tape it from the display screen, because a video recorder could not take the digital content of the CPU's composite signal without RF modulation.
5. The phone line modem may be used only for data communication and perhaps slow-scan images.
6. Transmission of the *total* video display must take place by standard fast-scan transmitting media or by manual transportation of the camera's output.

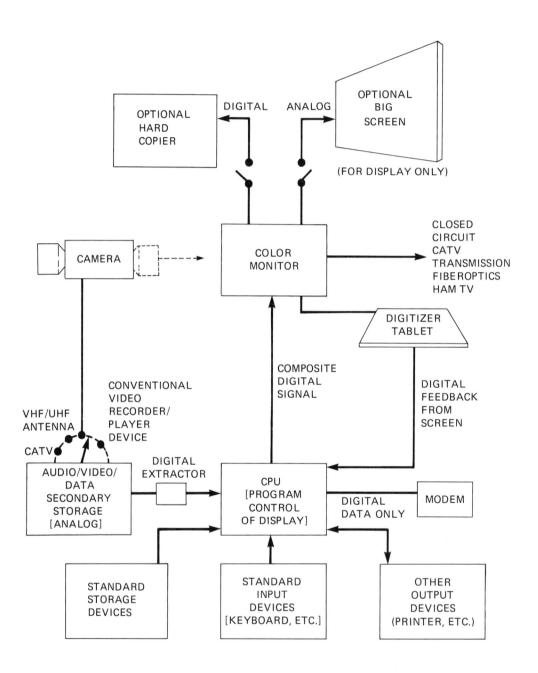

figure 4–21 The digital video/computer system, fully expanded.

7. In such a system, the display would probably be made of pixel or light-emitting diode (LED) elements, instead of phosphate groupings. However, a standard CRT with at least a 1,000 line resolution should be adequate to produce a quality, relatively "nondigitized" image.

A MORE REALISTIC
DIGITAL SYSTEM

Should the videodisc become user-recordable in a commonplace fashion in the near future, then you'd have to take a different approach. You would convert the analog input of a camera or TV monitor *before* storing it on the videodisc. In this manner, the video information need not be sampled in real-time, but rather at a rate that permits a high-quality digital equivalent of a fast-scan display. The playback could take place later at normal speeds. Figure 4–22 shows the full system:

1. The computer system is a normal one.
2. All input, either from the camera or any other source is digitized *before* storage on the (hypothetically) user-recordable disc. The buffer holds the video information in analog form until the relatively slow A/D converter can get it all onto the disc. The disc then becomes fully a computer peripheral—a universal storage medium for the computer. No other storage is necessary.
3. The disc player can then interface with the CPU directly, feeding it audio/video information in digital form.
4. Again, no SEG is necessary, since the display is then completely under the control of the program.
5. The image may be recorded from the screen by the camera or re-recorded by the same or different recorder/player in inputting as well as on the size of the buffer.
6. All transmissions would necessarily be through an RS-232C and modem to perhaps fiber optics or coax cable. Phone lines would, of course, strangulate the transmission.
7. Again, the display would have to be a high-quality CRT, pixel, or LED.

But the bubble main memory in Figure 4–19, the high-speed digital extractor in Figure 4–20, and the low-cost programmable disc in 4–23 are not yet available.

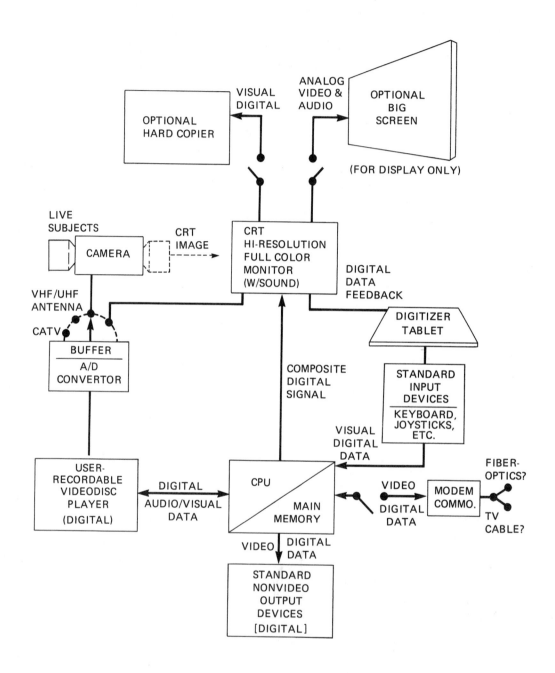

figure 4–22 A video/computer system with a user-recordable disc.

Systems utilizing digitized slow-scan images have many applications in business, security, medicine, education, and a number of other areas. The configuration shown in Figures 4–14 and 4–15 are useful any time a subject needs to be video recorded at such a distance that only phone lines or some other restricting medium is available. If a slow-scan does the job, then the system applies. Further, the videodisc (even in its read-only form) has gigantic potential in any situation that requires a great deal of interaction on a predeterminable basis. For example, students may use videodisc-based instruction modules to interact with the computer. The disc, with its quick random access, can branch into the necessary subroutines as warranted by the students' responses, possibly by voice command! The digital process of video storage holds great promise, should be pursued, and definitely should *not* be ignored.

The Analog System

At the present state of the art, the analog system is the easiest system to set up and the one that yields better results. Modulation seems to be cheaper and easier a process than digitizing—even though digitizing is not altogether expensive. For example, a unique chip set—LM1886/1889—from National Semiconductor Corp. permits home TVs to serve as computer terminals. These chips actually modulate incoming signals from VCRs, games, test equipment or similar sources, for display in black and white or color. The total cost of the two chips: under $5. The simple configuration in Figure 4–16 forms the basis for a more realistic expanded video/computer system, as shown in Figure 4–23. Notice several characteristics of this system:

1. It is generally more complicated and requires more equipment than digital layouts.

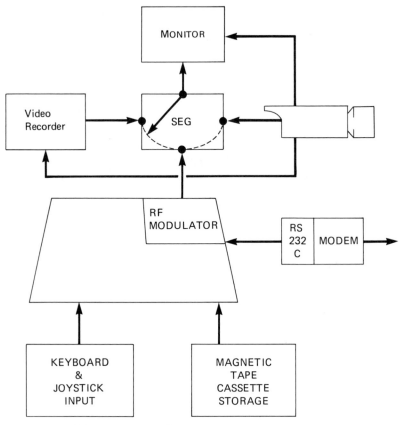

figure 4-23   A home or personal system.

2. An RF modulator must regulate the digital output of the CPU to the screen, if a home screen is being used to accommodate the video recorder. However, many home computers (TRS-80-II, Cromemco 2, Intellivision, Atari and others) already contain such a component; and surely the addition of one to an existing system should be neither costly nor troublesome.

3. A special effects generator (SEG) is necessary to switch and mix inputs, presumably under the normal control of the user at the computer systems input controls, at the controls of the SEG, or through a predetermined program read in from storage.

4. Only digital communication can be handled through the standard modem. The full video image can be communicated only through the normal media reserved for video band-widths. A less satisfactory, but probably more expedient, means is to record the display from the screen and send the tape on to the receiver by manual delivery.

174   The expanded layout is shown in Figure 4-24.

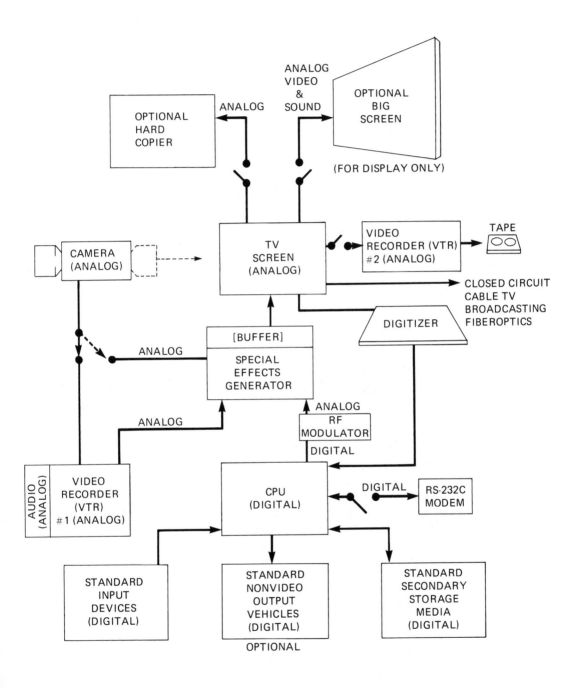

figure 4–24   An analog fast-scan integrated video/computer terminal, using existent equipment.

Why is the layout in Figure 4–22 the most practical choice? The answer to that question is the converse of the reason why a predominantly digital system is still a bit premature: The state of the art in either the video or the computer industry easily accommodates such a system. In a low-budget home or personal system, the user may already be utilizing a home terminal by means of a personal computer with a built in RF modulator. Disregarding options such as cameras, big screens, and screen printers, personal computerists need only a mixer of one degree of sophistication or another to blend video and data information (Figures 4–25 through 4–27). This essential component is likely the most expensive piece of equipment hobbyists have to purchase to integrate their video and computer systems.

figure 4–25 (a) Sharp's Color Sync Generator (XSG-370) is capable of driving five independent cameras. Its four subcarrier and four horizontal outputs are independently phase-adjustable from the front panel. The horizontal outputs may be either sync or horizontal drive. As a result, the system is capable of handling all kinds of cameras—or any combination of them—with external drive capability. Its suggested user net is $775.

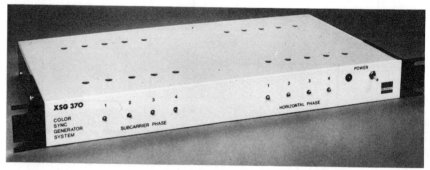

Courtesy: Sharp Electronics Corporation

Perhaps with some prescience, Intel surprised the computer world with general-purpose, analog microprocessor. The processor accepts analog signals, converts them to digital form, processes them digitally, and then sends the output off after conversion back into analog form—all on one chip! At a cost of $3,400, it holds great promise for IVTs of the future.

In larger, professional systems, the cash outlay is minimal, considering the potential of such a system. If a centralized

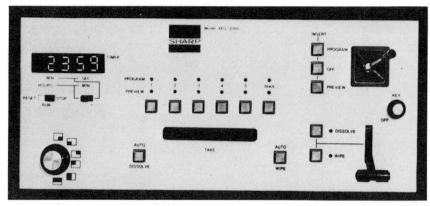

Courtesy:
Sharp Electronics
Corporation

figure 4–26 This professional special effects generator from Sharp has a built-in color sync generator, and phase shifter. The XSG-3000 adjusts phase without the use of electronic scopes. The suggested user net price is $2,900.

figure 4–27 These professional video switchers, available from Panasonic, enable a video user to switch among six inputs.

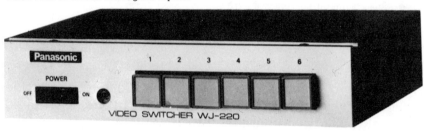

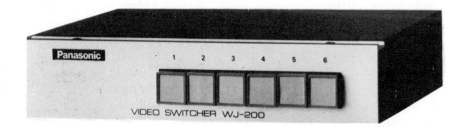

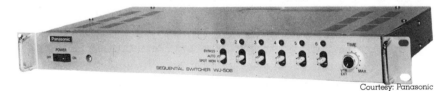

Courtesy: Panasonic

integrated station were situated so as to feed simple TV sets at remote locations, normal broadcasting or cable media could be used for fast-scan transmissions. This one-way type of station is rendered two-way as soon as the recipient decides to set up a similarly integrated terminal.

Which Way?

Analog? Digital? Mixers? Memories? SEGs? Which way will the technology go? Predicting or even extrapolating trends is difficult and often embarrassing. And, of course, no one can forecast a total breakthrough that could reverse trends overnight.

But generally the eighties promise to be digital. The fourteenth Annual Television Conference, held by the Society of Motion Picture and Television Engineers (SMPTE), divided its activities into four sessions:

- The Digital Television Plant
- Digital Signal Processing
- Digital Techniques
- Digital Recording

And in June of 1979, *Broadcast Communications* ran an article entitled "If It Isn't Digital, It Will Be." The article, by Harold Ennes states that, "within the next decade, the all-digital television plant will be a reality, making it very fast and far more flexible." Apparently only some of the audio people are unconvinced. At an Audio Engineering Society meeting in May of 1979 (as reported by the *Los Angeles Times*), convention vice chairman William Bauer stated: "There are some members of the society who really think that digital is going to dry up in a couple of years. There are others who think it's going to revolutionize the industry."

In either the analog or digital mode we are getting into a whole new sort of communication, with nearly limitless applications. Conceivably, a top executive of a national or even international organization could conference with area managers anywhere in the world in a kind of electronic meeting. Each participant could make a complete audio/visual/data record of the meeting, or with the appropriate equipment obtain hard copies of pertinent data during the conference. Medical consultations could be conducted in minutes and in great detail, even if the consulting physicians are at great distances from one another. X-rays, scans, test results, and other pertinent data—including a video picture of the patient—could be transmitted in moments and the recipient doctor totally briefed in minutes. In at least higher education, in which discipline and close supervision are not concerns of the instructor, such a terminal with simpler satellite stations could prove to be a most effective means of delivering a powerful audio/visual presentation to a lecture-sized course. In fact, class members need not even be in the same lecture hall or even on the same campus. Engineers working on the same project at different locations can meet and talk periodically, exchanging their information and cross-testing their ideas.

The applications are actually limitless and exciting. Our letter-writing, our phone-calling, our trips to special meetings, our report-writing, our check-writing, our passive TV-viewing, and most of our presently common activities—all of this the integrated video/computer renders tedious, quaint, and eventually obsolete.

Perhaps the most practical reason for developing an IVT is necessity. Right now—at this moment—some kind of integrated system is necessary to keep up with the decades-long explosion of information all over the world. Video graphics is not only faster because of its electronic nature; it is faster because it is visual. A person can "see" a conclusion, a trend, a situation, an idea faster in pictorial form than in verbal form. The combination of words and pictures—data and video information—in integrated systems that produce selective presentations on cue is a practical necessity. It is necessary today, and it becomes more so everyday. If a less-than-ideal configuration is the best we can do for whatever reasons, then that configuration should be utilized to the fullest, while better ones develop.

Summary

The integration of video and computer equipment is hampered not so much by the differing standards of manufacturers as it is by the essential differences between the way a video recorder stores information and the way a computer stores information. If the two technologies are to merge successfully, then the output of one must be made compatible with that of the other. One common form of storage—main or external—must be developed to handle the combined video of both. Since neither development is likely before the early or mid-eighties, we must for necessity's sake work with the components on hand and look forward to better systems in the future.

Assuming an individual or organization can start up an integrated video/computer terminal, then the next logical step is to link one such station with others in a free-for-all communications network. Communications, therefore, is the subject of the next chapter.

chapter **5**

The Communicator's Point of View

Unraveling the
Communications Knot

Imagine a bundle of computers and cameras, minis and modems, modulators and muxors, digitizers and data processors, teletext and telephones, TV and teleconferencing, fast scan and slow scan, satellites and storage—all cinched up precariously and haphazardly, Gordian style, by telephone wires, TV cables, and fiber optic lines. That's the "world" of communications today, which most people recognize as confusing at best. A "Viewpoint" in *Data Communications* (February 1978) stated:

> Data communications is so complex . . . that the question is raised whether any one person is capable of fully comprehending and exploiting all of the available technology, software, and networking concepts that are now current.

If the situation sounds discouraging, it's actually not as bad as it sounds. With today's video and home computer equipment at their disposal, hobbyists and "wireheads" all over the world have the potential of setting up full-scale integrated video terminals *right now*. All the capability is either on the market at ever-decreasing cost or on its way from several sources. And even the snarl in communications is about to unravel itself, a development that would put home computer/video enthusiasts in communication with one another just about overnight.

In fact, we are standing at the threshold of a whole new world of information handling and communication. Though historians may dicker about when the recording of information began, let's assume that people started writing things down about 4000 B.C. Some of them drew squiggles on papyrus with a brush or a crude pen. Some scribed wedge-shaped figures into wet clay; once dried, the clay became a permanent record. (Talk about casting your words in stone!) Over the millenia that followed, nothing very big happened to communications. Even though the printing press enabled books to be more widely circulated than ever before, the basic principle of physical "squiggles-on-a-flat-surface" remained the same. And producing a book still took time, which meant that its information aged even during the production process—a problem that the publishing industry is just beginning to confront. As revolutionary as was the printing press, it really does not represent much of a "leap" on the growth curve. In other words, the curve remained level and flat for thousands and thousands of years, with only minor innovations and variations on the basic principle. We were still writing squiggles on a flat surface.

But with the invention of the telegraph, the curve noses upward just a little. The telephone nudges the line up still a bit farther.

Then television, then computers, then photocopiers, and then a whole string of developments—in all directions and in quick succession—started an acceleration of the curve that shows no signs of slacking off. Right now—today—the many inventions and refinements of the past hundred years or so are starting to come together in such a way that they feed themselves. They generate knowledge and communication that, in turn, generates even more intense knowledge and communication. Approximately half of the American work force handles information in one form or another. Thus the curve bends upwards at an ever increasing rate. The latest developments in video and radio recording, in microelectronics, in computerization, and in social reactions to all this change are starting to come together into a system that will make each individual more aware of what is going on, more involved, and more effective in making things happen.

Communications today present us with a fork in the road of history. Think of it: the average citizen now has the advantages that a few years ago only large, well financed organizations had:

1. low-cost sophisticated data processing equipment,
2. high-quality sound and film recording devices,
3. personal, two-way interactive radio, TV, and video telephones,
4. instant home TV production and remote video retrieval,
5. long-distance sub-minute facsimiles,
6. world-wide satellite link-ups,
7. highly protective security and safety systems, and
8. self-supporting environmental controls and energy-generating techniques (solar power).

The consumer is ready to evaluate and, at the right price, possibly buy whatever the big manufacturer has to sell. In this case, the products give the consumer a latent power, a potential self-sufficiency, ultimately a control over what only large monied blocs could control before: the source, type and timing of entertainment, automated business management, calculating and information retrieval powers for research and development, energy, and so on.

Now, with the power hidden in the products, consumers/citizens need only coordinate their efforts to use this power to the general benefit of the public, to the overall good of the country. In order to communicate power, you need communication systems . . . personal network systems. Those that are now in expanding abundance—60 or more—are the communications links that can bring all these trends together. But first some remaining communications problems must be solved.

The Facts

At least certain facts regarding video/computer communications are clear:

1. A fast-scan, color video image requires a transmission bandwidth of at least 6 mHz.
2. Conventional broadcasting and cablecasting techniques accommodate this bandwidth.
3. As the bandwidth of a given transmission medium is narrowed, the transmission signal must be compressed and/or slowed down to fit into the medium. As a result, the scanning rate is stretched out, and the image usually becomes slow-scan or even freeze-frame.
4. Existing conventional telephone lines are capable of transmitting bandwidths that accommodate only human hearing—voice grade, 20 to 22,000 decibels. The phone line bandwidth is about 2.8 kHz.
5. Phone lines are capable of sending compressed slow-scan or freeze frame video signals, but no fast-scan pictures, because they can transmit at only a small fraction of the rate necessary for fast-scan TV. (The exception is AT&T's "dedicated lines." AT&T offered, in early 1981, a compression—or "splitting"—system that it says will provide slow- or fast-scan video communication.)

6. Phone lines have proved to be invaluable as a nascent communications network for computers. Through modems and acoustic couplers, computers have been able to take advantage of the existent system since some of their slower transmission requirements fit line specifications quite nicely. Data interchanged between computers may manifest itself at the terminal in CRT display. Insofar as the data streams have already given rise to a video presentation, then computer communications may be considered a facet of video communications.

Given these facts as starting points, perhaps the clearest method of approach is to take each level of either video, computer, or video/computer communications in turn and discuss its relation to the integrated video/computer terminals.

Data Transmission
Over Phone Lines

Of all forms of video or computer communications, except conventional broadcasting or cablecasting, telephone data communications is probably the simplest and most common. In early 1980, sixty personal computer systems were setting up computer networks for the enhancement of their database and message system needs. On a larger scale, institutions and businesses all over the world are arranging electronic "handshaking" agreements for up-to-the-minute dissemination of information. Throughout the industry, the overall trend is conspicuously in favor of ditigalization. Analog transmissions are giving way more and more to more versatile, faster, and more reliable compressed, digital data transmission and reception.

Modems and Acoustic
Couplers

To integrate a computer into a network or to connect it with another computer, all an end user needs is either an acoustic coupler or a modem. Either instrument is simply a piece of hardware that interfaces the computer to the phone, allowing the computer's data stream to carry through the phone lines. Fundamentally the modem at the transmitting station (the modulator) accepts digital output from a processor and provides *185*

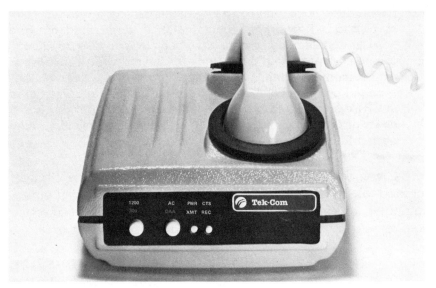

figure 5–1   The Tek-Com 3003 is a full-duplex, asynchronous 0- to 1,200-baud modem for voice-grade telephone lines. It is compatible with all computer systems and data terminals using Bell 103 handshakes.

analog audio-frequency signals for transmission. With a *multi-plexor*, a user can feed several such signals into one higher-speed line. The modem at the receiving terminal (the demo-dulator) reconverts these signals into digital pulses. Modems are often also called "data sets," "data-communications equip-ment (DCE)," "data-circuit terminating equipment," or "binary serial DCEs." The whole process is another instance of the essential difference between the computer and the world around it.

Types.   The general categories are:

1. voice-grade (VG) modems and telephone couplers,
2. wideband modems,
3. short-haul modems, and
4. modem eliminators or line driver/receivers.

The most common by far are those used on the voice-grade telephone lines with 2.7 kHz effective bandwidths (300 Hz to 3kHz). Modem selection for VG lines depends on several consid-erations, such as:

186

1. whether the service is dial-up, leased, or Bell System compatible;
2. data rates;
3. error rates.

Many modem types and brands do not work together, but Bell System modems or their equivalents from independent manufacturers work together. So Bell compatibility is an important modem feature for system integration.

Modems (modulator/demodulator) can be used to accept data or command input over practically any kind of communications or data transmission system. The function of an acoustic coupler is similar to that of a modem, with the primary exception that the audio signal is transmitted acoustically through a standard telephone set, rather than electrically, as in the case of codec chip sets or a hard-wired modem. In effect, these devices bring together digital equipment with analog lines.

The way this function is accomplished varies considerably from one designer to another and also with new components as they become available. Many technical improvements have been made during the last decade and they will no doubt continue as technology advances and practical problems are solved. Either type of device generally uses two separate frequency bands for transmission and reception. In the Bell 103 modem, for instance, 1070 Hz and 1270 Hz are used to send, while 2025 and 2225 are used to receive.

Acoustic couplers, rather than modems, have helped the growth of the timesharing market because they are cheap, simple, and portable. This market has rapidly expanded in terms both of applications and the wide variety of remote terminals in use today. One report indicated that by the end of 1978, a little under 300,000 low-speed (300 baud, 30 characters per second) and approximately 9,000 high speed (1,200 baud, 120 characters per second) couplers were installed. Transmission at a faster rate (120 characters/second) has created a growing demand for 1,200-baud couplers.

Previously, in addition to either the modem or coupler, most telephone company tariffs required an adaptor on the phone line, which was rented from the phone company. The adaptor ensured that the telephone company did not have feedback to its lines. Adaptors are now built into many modems and other equipment.

Protocols. Computers in a network must all use an agreed-upon *protocol*, or format, for their data. Various protocols refer to baud rates and the configuration of such things as headers, data blocks, and error detection and correction techniques, etc. These formats should also be compatible with or convertible to the formats used by mass storage devices such as floppy disks. A simplified data communication layout is shown in Figure 5–2.

figure 5–2   A simplified, two-station network. While adaptors are sometimes available from phone companies on an optional basis, others insist that they be used to insure proper input matching. They also serve to inform the phone company that your line to the central switcher must be of uniform data transmission quality. Some phone lines are not computer-transmission grade. A few of these Personal Computer NETworks (PCNETs) are already in operation, and we will discuss them in this chapter.

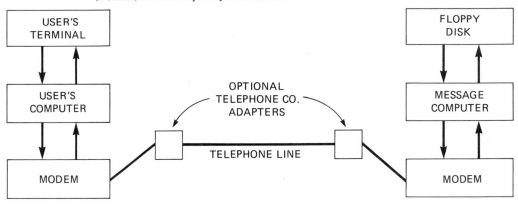

Most computers are equipped with interfaces, or microprocessor "front ends," that are programmed to accept many protocol types as well as messages from many different kinds of equipment. Whether a modem or acoustic coupler is used, another device should have enough software control to dial and to answer the phone—an important consideration for entering a computer into network.

Transmission Modes and Techniques

Modes.   When planning for the transmission of data over phone lines, between computers, terminals, or other communication interfaces, users should decide whether the mode will be simplex, half-duplex, or full duplex. *Simplex transmission* means that the data may travel in one direction only; a simplex is a one-way line, such as those that run to "slave" terminals or from one-way sources. *Half-duplex* lines allow transmission in both directions but not simultaneously. *Full duplex transmission* takes place in two directions at the same time.

Techniques.   Further, the transmission technique is either asynchronous or synchronous. *Asynchronous transmission* takes place in irregular bursts, without regard for the "timing" of the receiver hardware. The time interval between successive characters' signals, bursts or strings varies. The receiver hardware recognizes the beginning and end of a transmission only by means of a standardized set of beginning and ending characters—"start" and "stop" bits. *Synchronous transmission*, on the other hand, is a timed transmission that "beats" (so to speak) in rhythm with the timing of the receiver hardware. As minute as the interval between signals may be, this type of transmission eliminates the lag that occurs in asynchronous technique.

Synchronous transmission, with its sometimes greater efficiency, is often used for high-speed communication applications; the asynchronous technique is sometimes used for the lower speeds, 2,000 bps (bits per second) or less. Asynchronous units operate at maximum data rates of 1,800 bps over dial-up lines and at 2,000 bps on "conditioned" leased lines. The top rate for synchronous units is 4,800 bps over dial-up lines and 9,600 bps over leased lines.

Transmission Quality

Besides making sure that the phone company gives you data transmission quality service (often in the form of special "dedicated" lines), you can take a few measures to ensure quality transmission. Although data pulses are subject to noise on a distortion in the lines, whose quality is generally considered to be lower than the average audio cassette, such interference can normally be cleared up at repeater stations. Hope for better transmission in the future lies with AT&T's experiments with fiber optics cables. Voice and data transmissions are digitized and beamed along hairline glass filaments. Since light waves *189* have a greater bandwidth than radio or electrical waves, more information can be sent by flexible optical tubes. Besides increased capacity, fiber optic lines are immune to electrical interference and much smaller and lighter than the existent copper lines.

Codecs

The A/D/D/A dilemma is rapidly disappearing due to an apparently cut-and-dried aspect of computer communications. In the wake of increasing use of the phone network for data communications, telecommunications has rapidly moved toward the conversion of voice (analog) signals to digital form with PCM, an early popular method. Converted into a *serial data* stream, voice signals are *more easily manipulated:* the data can be *compressed* for *extremely high speed transmission* without the loss of integrity that analog transmissions suffer. Further, if data streams corresponding to individual voice signals are ordered into specific time slots—or time domain multiplexed—the interconnection of two circuit paths can be carried out essentially in software: computers at each end simply agree on a common time slot. In short, all-digital switching will, in time, supplant the electromechanical cross-reed switches that switch the bulk of today's phone conversations.

Preceding all-digital switching is the codec (coder-decoder). It consists of an A/D coder on the sending end of the line and a D/A decoder at the receiving end. The use of one D/A converter in the coding section and another in the decoding section has several advantages. Two coders improve performance, because the isolation between the transmitting and receiving circuitry greatly exceed that of the more common shared-converter approach. For another, it makes the device easier to use, because the transmitting and receiving sections are separate and can even be clocked at different rates.

Developments and devices leading up to all-digital switching are very promising. AT&T and many other national networks are well on their way to switching entire phone networks over to digital transmission. The powerful Data Encryption Standard (DES) chip, for example, automatically enciphers plain text into encrypted transmissions that are unintelligible to intruders. The key is electronically stored and transmitted;

suppliers advertise that no human "can ever know or determine exactly which key is in use." There is technological reason for holding up this abrupt change; economically its advent is imperative for practically all potential users, consumers, industry, governments, and others. Only bureaucratic lethargy can delay the oncoming digital communication revolution.

Packet Switching

One common form of data transmission is to transmit data in packets. In a packet system, data enters a network via a multiplexor at the computer site or on local phone loops. The multiplexor then breaks up the data into blocks or packets, each accompanied by destination and origin addresses. In packets, a header tells certain things about the data such as its type, source, destination, length, and so on. Then a block, containing the actual data, followed by a checksum to test the validity of the transmission, follows. The destination computer receives the packet, performs a checksum, and, if the data is intact, copies the packet into its memory. Meanwhile the sending computer waits to receive acknowledgement from the destination computer that the packet has been received and was not lost or garbled. Source computers send streams of miscellaneous packets. The packets can be processed by the receiving computer immediately or stored for eventual use at the user's discretion. As the data stream passes through each network connection point (or node), locally destined packets are pulled out and the rest sent on to the next node. The packet switching system is an electronic and elaborate "take-yours-and-pass-the-rest-on" system. In another sense, it is merely a long-distance extension of a front-end processor.

Advantages. Packet switching is a serious contender for dominance in the telecommunications market. Compared to conventional telephone or specialized data lines, the packet network sets up connections faster, monitors errors and other transmission problems through diagnostic software, and reduces the cost of certain types of data transmission. Packet nets also make conferences among interactive terminal users a lot easier, and permit program and file transfers between host computers and other multiple or simultaneous data links. The packet network can also store and forward packets when a host is ready to accept data, and even small computers can be readily programmed to take on more functions as needed. Packet systems avoid most of the conventional switching nodes that create data errors on the telephone network. Since the route of each packet is not determined in advance, any route can be used to minimize expense and traffic congestion. And packets are automatically checked at each node and retransmitted if in error or if receipt has not been properly acknowledged.

All this action happens in a fraction of a second. Although seemingly complex, it is all invisible to the user. Also, the code conversions features enable a wide range of dissimilar equipment to be interfaced without causing users to buy special hardware or complex software routines. In short, a packet network can be "plug-compatible" with practically any computer device.

Perhaps the primary advantage of packet switching is that it is economical. Packet switching provides a lower cost integrated network for digital voice and data communications operations than do many standard and hybrid circuit-switching arrangements. Aside from satellites, the costs of some network alternatives to packet-switching range from 30 to over 1,700 percent higher than packet switching.

PACKET NETWORKS

Commercial packet networks run by GTE, Telenet, Tymnet, and Graphnet emerged in the late 70's following the original government-run Arpanet system. The Com-Pak network, under development by ITT, and the Advanced Communications System, a Bell System data service, are also believed to involve some packet techniques.

As software and new packet switches are unveiled by Digital Communications Corporation and Telenet, major corporations are implementing or at least considering private packet networks. Some major corporate telecommunications users are integrating voice communications into their packet plans. Western Union International, for example, entered into

an agreement with Telenet in July of 1977. WUI's international communications network is connected to Telenet's domestic network to enable subscribers to utilize, via Telenet, WUI's Database Service that was inaugurated earlier in 1977 in the United Kingdom. Database Service can access computers in other countries for database information and for remote computing. Also, users in other countries can access information retrieval services in the US, such as the National Library of Medicine's "Medline" and Lockheed's "Dialog." WUI said it has plans to expand its Database Service to all of the major countries in Europe. Telenet also furnishes turnkey, packet-switched data communication systems for private networks.

THE HARDWARE

The private network systems utilize a line of microprocessor equipment and software developed by Telenet for its own nationwide common carrier network. The turnkey network support the accepted worldwide standard protocol for packet networks (CCITT X.25) and can be linked to X.25-based public networks such as Telenet in the United States and other networks around the world. The cornerstone of its private network is the TP 4000. This unit is a packet-switching network node as a network access concentrator for data terminals and computer systems. With plug-in network interface, it requires no changes to the user's existing data equipment or software.

Telenet also supplies a minicomputer-based network control center as part of its private network offering. To connect to the Telenet network, the TP 4000 requires one or more synchronous access lines, depending on the traffic load and redundancy requirements. When two or more access lines are used, the traffic is automatically distributed among the lines to level peak loads and minimize queuing delays. The flow control feature enables asynchronous ports at the host end of a connection to operate at speeds up to 9,600 bits per second while terminals at the remote end operate at any speed from 50 to 9,600 bits per second.

Packet switching has also taken to the radio airwaves. A system of packet-switched microprocessor-controlled radio data links routes tactical messages from one node to another for military field operations. Packets of data with identifying headers and error-correcting trailers are broadcast from a main *193* station and routed independently and asynchronously throughout the system. Actual transmission is spread over a wideband of frequencies to provide special safeguards against jamming and eavesdropping.

Computer Networks

Owners of institutional databases for computers have been awaiting widespread computer networks for many years. For example, scores of nonprofit firms operate computer databases. One typical system is used by 1,500 librarians in 47 states. Bell Labs, Lockheed, Time-Life, The New York Times, Merrill-Lynch—among many, many others—are all building huge databases, and they contemplate more widespread and profitable use for them. It's about time, then, that personal computing enthusiasts generated their own networks and also tapped in on these larger databases (Figure 5–3).

figure 5–3   The VuSet Data Terminal, the Alpha/Numeric keyboard, and a standard telephone provide a complete telecommunication terminal capability.

Courtesy:
Bell Laboratories

PCNET. The Personal Computing Network (PCNET) is such a project. Started in 1977 by a group of professional computerists, the network was developed by people "in the industry" who worked on the project in their spare time. The only requirements for participation are:

1. a personal computer with 12 to 16 K of RAM and string BASIC, and
2. an originate/answer modem capable of 300 bps.

figure 5-4   The four models of the Astra Series of small business computers range in size from a one-CRT station with 128KB memory to a 32-station system with a main memory of up to 512KB. Integrated applications sofware includes sales order processing, sales analysis, inventory control, accounts receivable, accounts payable, general ledger, and payroll for the first-time computer user.

Courtesy:
Nippon Electronic
Corporation

MicroNET.   CompuServe's system offers the following:

1. communication with other small computer users,
2. the ability to buy and sell software through the network,
3. practical personal programs,
4. educational aids,
5. easy and advanced programming languages, and
6. games.

To join the network, all you need is a personal computer or computer terminal and a telephone. MicroNET users can also   *195* access large-scale computer systems in off-peak hours, from 6 in the evening to 5 in the morning on weekdays and all day on weekends and most holidays. Besides a one-time sign-up charge of $9, users pay $5 per hour user charges, payable by Master Charge.

For more information, write:

Compu Serve, Inc.
Personal Computing Division
5000 Arlington Centre Boulevard
Columbus, Ohio

Source. Perhaps the most popular personal computer network, Source offered users seven BASIC commands when it started up, with more to follow in time. The charge for message service was 4.6 cents per minute. The only extra charge in late 1979 was for filing, billed after midnight of the day of the message; that charge was a mere 3.3 cents per day per 2,000 characters.

For more information, write:

Telecomputing Corporation of America
1616 Anderson Road
McLean, Virginia 22102

Video Data Transmission Over the Air Waves

Just as digital data is compressed to send faster audio signals through the phone lines, the Air Force has developed a data compression technique that sends a TV signal from a missile to a ground base. The purpose of the system is twofold: to transmit a video signal with a bandwidth less than that required for an ordinary TV signal, and second to preclude jamming. Since 80 percent of the picture has to be eliminated in the A/D conversion, a microcomputer must control which elements are decorded and which retained. A 256 × 256 frame is the end result
(Figure 5–5).

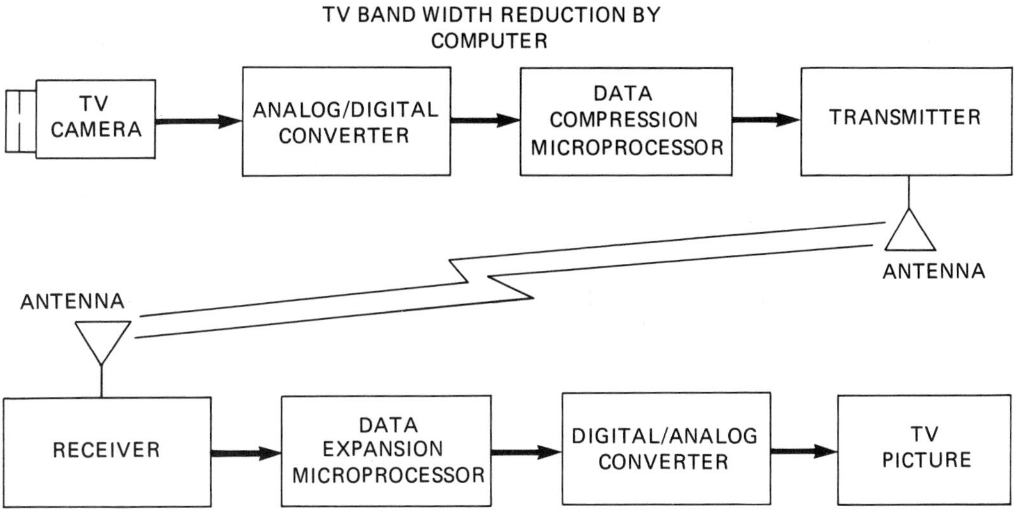

TV BAND WIDTH REDUCTION BY
COMPUTER

figure 5–5 A microprocessor compresses a signal from a TV camera by rejecting redundant parts of the picture. At the receiver end, the reverse process occurs, again under microprocessor control.

The same principle is used in HAM TV, covered in Chapter 2. Slow-scan amateur TV (SSTV) is a low-resolution, narrow-bandwidth video transmission technique characterized by approximately a thousand-to-one reduction in bandwidth from conventionally broadcast TV. SSTV has a bandwidth of about 3 kHz, which is suitable for storage on tape recorders and for transmission by individual radio transmittors. Titling is usually accomplished by character generators under computer program control. The microprocessor has to be a slave to the scan converters. The vertical and horizontal pulses provide a synchronization basis for integration with the CPU. The configuration for transmitting is shown in Figure 5–6, and the interface card is shown in Figure 5–7. For black-and-white slow-scan pictures, such a system is an adequate video/computer terminal onto itself.

Such is the interest in amateur broadcasting that personal computerists may soon be able to receive information and advertising via digital broadcasting over an FM carrier. The Digicast Project was in its preparatory stages in early 1978, a time when Jim Warren, Jr. (the director of the program) expressed the feeling that regionally broadcast advertising would be a more efficient medium for local retailers.

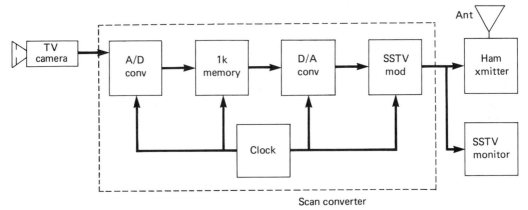

figure 5–6 A scan converter.

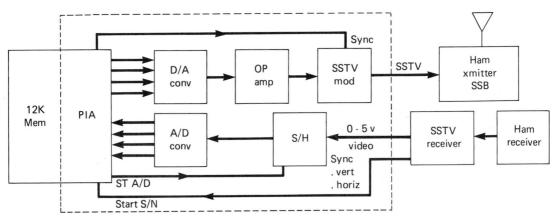

figure 5–7 An SSTV interface card.

Facsimile Transmission or Electronic Mail

Although electronic mail is not strictly a video/computer component, it can very likely become a factor that will enable small computer owners to communicate more openly and quickly than ever before. Ultimately, as adjuncts to computer systems, electronic mail devices will communicate either the hard-copy output of a fax or plotter or the digital data from a word processor. In effect, electronic mail represents an outgrowth of

198

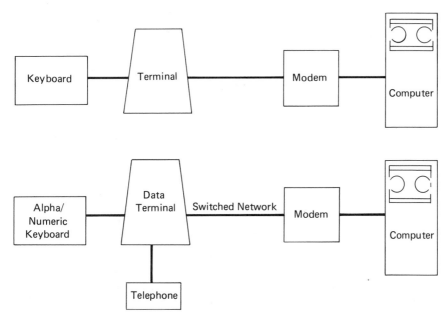

figure 5-8

many techniques of electronic information communication. In the past, paper information handling was conducted through the ancient, inefficient, slow, expensive mail system or delivery service. Quicker communication was accomplished over the phone, but this was "non-record" and unsatisfactory. Now hard copies (records) can be sent in seconds over one phone, without the necessity for people to converse over another.

A quick way of transmitting pictures and documents in hard-copy form is nothing more than the electronic version of the Post Office. *Electronic mail* is any system that produces a hard-copy communication at the receiver's end that duplicates exactly the original on the transmitter's end. Although not part of the definition, speed is inherent in any electronic communication system, as compared to hard-copy mailing systems. Electronic mail and messages systems (EMMS) can really take two forms: the first is the high speed communication of digital data over any kind of transmission medium (cable, radio, phone, satellite) that normally can carry digital information. Usually this kind of information (message) is now under computer control and often involves computer-to-computer interaction; a printer or copier at the receiving end plays out the hard-   *199* copy (mail) output of the digital transmission. The second type is strictly EM: facsimile transmission, or fax, which is basically a stretched-out photocopier system. The simple scanning device is at the transmitting end, and the reproducing device is at the receiving end. Transmission is accomplished through a modem (often a built-in card) and the phone lines or microwaves and satellites.

Large corporations and small enterprises alike are now turning toward electronic mail more and more, as harried executives find themselves waiting three days for "guaranteed" overnight mail from the Post Office:

1. In 1978, ITT Domestic Communications Transmission Service, Incorporated was working out software snags in an ambitious "interface to any machine" facsimile network. The "Faxpak" service began November, 1980.

2. Southern Pacific's Communications was working on a centrally switched network as part of their Speed Fax service. The switching center is designed to operate as a store-and-forward center. A fax terminal should cost under $50 per month, a fee that includes 20 pages of transmission on some contracts. Incremental rates are scheduled as low as 10 cents per page.

3. The Quip fax rented for $29/month in 1979, and Qwix System (a division of Exxon) is a typewriter that can be made into an electronic mail terminal.

4. The 3M company was marketing its "20-second" Express 9600, a microcomputer-controlled digital transceiver console that also has automatic, anytime dialing and document feed. Its transmission can be sent over conventional phone lines.

5. Panafax Corporation puts out, among a long line of products, the MV-1200, a facsimile transceiver that works well with most other fax communications equipment. Before transmitting copy, for instance, the MV-1200 queries the receiving terminal as to transmission speed, mode selection, line quality, phasing, paper supply, and so on. When the transmission is completed, the receiver equipment signals a verification, and both ends hang up the phone and return to standby.

To indicate the imminent popularity of electronic mail, consider this: Nippon Telegraph and Telephone Public Corporation decided in 1978 to go after the low-end of the facsimile market with home telecopiers. It was shipping units by early 1979. Consider that, in the spring of 1978, only one company

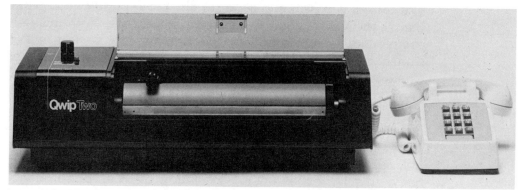

figure 5-9   Qwip is a simple machine that sends words and pictures over phone lines, anywhere you can make a phone call.   Courtesy: Exxon Enterprises, Inc.

was reported as offering a system economical enough for the small business owner to afford, while that one year saw still another postal rate increase without a concomitant increase in service but rather the threat of a walk-out strike. The small businessperson has every right to look forward to a large array of electronic mail devices in the eighties.

Typical of a global fax transmission system is RCA's Q-Fax. Q-Fax is a digital facsimile service introduced in May of 1977,

figure 5-10   Sent only ten seconds ago from Tokyo, a copy of an 8 1/2 × 11″ facsimile message is ready on RCA's Q-fax.

Courtesy: RCA

that makes it possible to send an 8½ × 11" page of copy from San Francisco to Japan in less than 26 seconds. With this new commercial facsimile service, documents can be transmitted overseas in tongues that do not use Roman letters—such as Chinese, Arabic, Japanese—without the need to translate. It permits users to send and receive printed or handwritten messages, legal briefs, contacts, computer printouts, schematic drawings or shipping waybill forms between RCA's Q-Fax center in San Francisco and the Kokusai Denshin Denwa Co., Ltd. (KDD) international communications center in Tokyo. Initially, this high-speed, high-resolution $10 per page service provided a much needed communications medium between the United States and Japan, but RCA's management expanded this service to other overseas countries such as Australia and others by late 1979, with many more to come. The service to Japan can be initiated by delivering a facsimile message to RCA Globcom's Office at One Market Plaza in San Francisco. This can be by messenger, by facsimile sent over a leased line to RCA's operating center or over the local public telephone network. It is also possible to initiate a message by using a

figure 5–11 Telautograph is a company that produces a long line of communications devices that transmit hand-drawn or hand-written messages via the phonelines. In this photo are shown the DY11 Transmitter (right). On the Memo Transmitter, the person simply handwrites a message as he or she would do normally for company distribution or mailing. But in this case, the touch of the pen starts the transmission of the corresponding digital data that moves the scribe on the same device at the receiving end, reproducing the writer's handwriting exactly.

Courtesy:
Telautograph

202

domestic communications carrier interconnected with RCA Globcom's Q-Fax service.

Such systems, like data transmissions, really do not lend themselves to video/computer applications as we have defined them. More to the point is the ability to communicate video images from one video/computer terminal to another.

Teleshopping:
Electronic Funds Transfer (EFT)

With ever more working women and two-income families, people have less and less time to spend at shopping centers. By sometime in the middle or late 1980s, people are likely to stop going out to shop, and so the stores are going to have to go to the shoppers. As consumers desire additional convenience in shopping, shop-at-home systems will be the answer. (The energy crisis might just be the catalyst that brings this scenario into the very near future—instead of some ten or more years down the road.)

Shopping by TV cable is coming for sure, especially because it is so easy. Advertisers simply offer products, purchasers punch their terminal with selections, credit or debit card numbers, and delivery is the next day—or even within a few hours, if requested. The Qube systems can do this now, and CATV companies that have head-end computers could easily offer the same service. And the many extra channels on most CATV systems could be used for special shopping services.

The *Home Terminal Report* (developed by the New York research firm, Frost & Sullivan, in March, 1979) stated: "The implementation of bill payments via home terminals by financial institutions will become the fastest growing electronic funds transfer service during the 1980s." The report also said, "We are just entering the introductory phase of a home terminal market. The opportunities are enormous for development of a wide range of new services and products." How big is this market? "At-home bill payment represents one of the most important of the new transaction services. More than 4,000 financial institutions will offer such bill payment services by 1989. By then, some 1,535 systems will be installed throughout the U.S.—up from 75 installations recently."

In another article from the June 1979 issue of *Electronics Business* (page 87):

> A few years ago most people laughed at the idea of paying bills by telephone. Now more than 100 banks offer the service and it's hard to find a city where it's not becoming a consumer demand.
>
> Tangney says First Boston's system will answer the dialed codes with a verbal message, such as "Thank you for paying Boston Edison $42.50; your account has been debited a total of $287.50. Thank you." The computer will effect the funds transfer from the individual's accounts and print a monthly statement to describe the transactions in detail. Most bank customers who've tried the service agree it's a better way of paying bills. The future of telephone funds services seems assured.
>
> As customers catch on to the many possibilities of electronic funds transfer, they will demand even more services from banks and retail stores. New ventures offering funds management services for fees will undoubtedly spring up. These will be independent businesses or subsidiaries of stores and banks.

From which direction does teleshopping come? Perhaps the major push comes from the banks seeking to capture consumers' dollars faster and more efficiently for their own purposes. The July 1979 issue of *The Videocassette & CATV Newsletter* reported:

> Work is proceeding to develop a viable method for consumers to pay bills from home via two-way cable television. According to *The EFT Report*, planners in the savings bank industry are moving closer to a test of such a service. They soon hope to bring home banking plus home catalog shopping to a small group of cable-tv subscribers in the New York City area. Each home in the experiment would be outfitted with a microprocessor-driven computer terminal with a keyboard hooked up to a tv set, and the incoming and outgoing cable. In addition to the funds transfer experiment, plans call for later tests of security services and access to airline reservations systems. The two-way cable experiment was conceived by MINTS (Mutual Institutions National Transfer System) the research and development arm of the National Association of Mutual Savings Banks.

Or perhaps the credit card phenomenon will give it a push. American Express is willing to invest several hundred millions of dollars not just in the two-way entertainment advantages of the Qube cable system (formerly entirely owned by Warner Communications, Inc.), but also in their successful "gift business" in association with its credit card systems. As Qube expands from city to city, certainly the two-way teleshopping American Express Credit Card Division will get a real "workout." Just as soon as Qube offers teleshopping, scores of other cable companies are bound to follow; the field is too lucrative to miss out.

Computer Conferencing

To this point, the chapter has been concerned with the transmission of data from one terminal to another. Transmission, although rather flexible thanks to satellites and packet-switching, was not always so coordinated that more than two people could participate.

Computer conferencing is a step beyond simple data transmission. At its computer-to-computer level, it is like a transcribed form of a telephone conference call. A computer conference consists of a group of people typing messages in their terminals and reading on a display screen or on a printout, what one or many other people are saying. The computer automatically informs the conference group when someone joins or leaves. When a computer signs off, it marks its location in the discussion and picks up at that point when it rejoins the conference.

Computer conferencing differs from eye-to-eye, verbal meetings in important ways. For one, the people engaged in a computer conference can be both geographically and chronologically spread out. Everyone may "talk" or "listen" at once. A person can make a contribution to the discussion at his or her own convenience, rather than having to wait until other speakers have finished. Members can work at their own paces taking as much or as little time as necessary to read, think, or reply. Each message is assigned a number and labeled with author, date, and time for easy identification and retrieval.

Sure input can be anonymous, discussions are more open and uninhibited. The results of votes are presented only as   *205* distributions and determining who voted which way is impossible when designed to be so. In addition, conferees can change their vote at any time. During the computer conference individuals may electronically "whisper" to one another by exchanging private messages, which do not become part of the permanent record of the conference. Other members are not even aware that these exchanges are taking place. The printout capability provides a permanent record of the proceedings and insures against misquoting. Receiving "keyword-subject" information without going through the entire text is also possible.

Computer conferencing also puts psychological pressure on anyone who tends to be verbose or irrelevant. No one is forced to pay attention to such people. In a face-to-face conference, other members have to fake interest in the speaker, but you cannot force anyone to read your messages. Finally, computer conferencing efficiently handles large group discussions involving twenty-five or more people such as "delphi" types. A conference telephone call begins to get difficult with more than five people, and face-to-face meetings encounter problems when more than fifteen are involved.

Computer conferencing, therefore, is a network of computer users—friends, associates, or anybody—who "get together" on various computers for purposes of discussion. The meeting is at anybody's convenience, and a "speaker" cannot be interrupted. It is communications purely on the personal level. No video is involved at all.

Video Conferencing

Electronic mail systems, as noted, still do not deliver anything but a hard-copy picture. The real advance will occur when a fast-scan image can be broadcast for teleconferencing at a rate that makes the service usable by everyone, including the low-budgeted small business operator, and even the individual computerist. Until that time, slow-scan video will have to do.

Video teleconferencing is any situation in which two or more people in different locations see and talk with each other through video equipment. Video transmission can be via phone line, radio wave, satellite, or other means. The primary objective of video conferencing is to cut down on travel time. If a busy university administrator must attend a seminar before lunch and meet with two colleagues in two different cities in the afternoon, he or she can make the seminar in person and teleconference with the colleagues. Critics of teleconferencing have discounted its worth, claiming that its value is no greater than a simple phone conference. Its proponents have brushed aside such objectives, answering that early computer-assisted instructional programs were of "little" significance also, primarily because they were still crude and formative.

In general, despite its high cost, people in business agree that teleconferencing at least serves its designated purpose of saving travel time. They are further fairly certain that teleconferencing speeds up decision making, thus expediting the running of a business. Satellite Business Systems' (SBS) Project Prelude experiment of 1978 uncovered several opinions among business managers:

1. Nearly three-quarters of those asked said teleconferencing beats traveling. The reduced traveling time and improved decision making were cited as chief benefits.
2. Sixty-two percent would encourage their company's implementation of a teleconferencing set-up.
3. Sixty-one percent didn't mind at all the freeze frame nature of the video, saying it was quite adequate for business meetings.

Obviously, teleconferencing has many applications outside the business world. People in business will seize upon any idea that reduces expenses and boring travel. They are therefore the pace-setters for video communications. And, as the SBS survey showed, they like it.

As much as it seems a desirable alternative to travel, video conferencing is expensive and relatively inaccessible. Most of the systems are private, and the public services are restricted. For example, AT&T's PicturePhone Service is available in only eleven cities in late 1979. Another, more intangible objection is that teleconferencing requires that all the old rules of meeting be rewritten. Just "hooking up" people electronically does not necessarily satisfy normal meeting protocols and/or the psychological needs of the people at the meeting. The "in-person" factor is missing.

figure 5-12   AT&T's PicturePhone Meeting Service is complete and automatic.

THE PROCESS

Whatever its consequences on the people involved, video conferencing adds a kind of "presence" to computer conferencing. Unfortunately, the video and the computer aspects of communication seem to be developing separately, if not away from each other. Presently, communications can consist completely of either video content (teleconferencing) or data content (network and computer conferencing), but no system combines the two in a single transmission medium, between individual integrated terminals, for a unified presentation. Therefore, perhaps a glimpse at how the video conference works will show how easily it could be enlarged to include computer transmissions.

Most video conferencing systems use the same fundamental process as the HAM slow-scan TV amateur (Figure 5-7). In the HAM process, one frame of the moving video image is "grabbed" by what is basically an A/D converter. The signal to start transmitting a frame may be under program or manual control. On the transmitting end, the frame is digitized and then compressed for narrow bandwidth transmission; at the receiving end, the signal is expanded for a slow-scan picture.

The basic process is true for both closed-circuit television (CCTV) as well as for phone line televison (PLTV), even though the resultant images differ. While CCTV offers a higher-resolution picture, its signal is good for only a certain length of cable, and then it starts breaking down. PLTV, with a poorer image, retains most or all of its signal quality regardless of the distance of transmission.

Closed circuit television generally utilizes a cable that can handle an 8-kHz transmission path. When it uses such a cable, the video equipment may be connected directly to the cable.

figure 5–13   Various CCTV configurations.

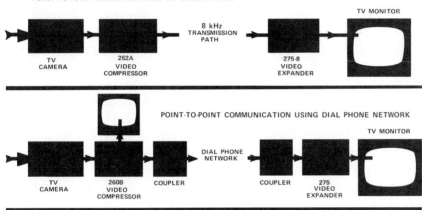

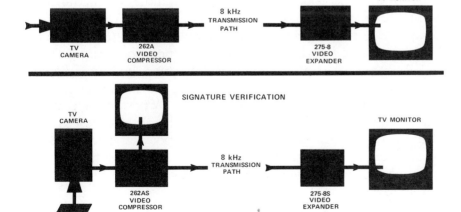

When a closed circuit is obliged to make use of existing phone lines, a coupler must be positioned between the video equipment and the line at both the transmission and reception points. The "compressor" and "expander," essentially one-in-the-same device, is an A/D/D/A converter with a twist. The twist is a memory slip that collects the digitized frame and shoots out the bit stream at a rate permitted by the line being used. In other words, "compressed" video is only "slowed-down," video— digitized and then released as the communications medium allows.

A typical compressor/expander set-up is Colorado Video's Model 260B Compressor and its Model 275 Expander. The model 260B Video Compressor converts standard television signals from a camera into narrow bandwidths for transmission over voice-grade communications circuits. Only still pictures are transmitted, with a typical frame time of 78 seconds per image for a medium resolution of 256 × 512 picture elements. A companion device, the Model 275 Video Expander (Figure 5–14) must be used at the receiving location to reconstruct the television image.

The 260B may be used with the normal "dial up" telephone network, leased lines, radio links, microwave, or satellite channels to provide low cost visual communications. Signals may also be easily recorded on conventional audio tapes or cassettes for later playback.

Features of the 260B include a small remote control panel for convenience in operation. This panel allows the user to select from three separate video input signals, to initiate or to terminate a transmission at any time, and to "pause" in the middle of a transmission for split screen effects. Control of an optional "frame freezing" device is also incorporated.

As a special set-up aid, the 260B produces a unique display on the associated TV monitor. The user is provided with a video waveform display superimposed over the TV image, thus allowing optimum adjustment of video signal levels and assessment of input quality as well as picture composition and focus. A vertical cursor also shows the degree of completion of the transmission as it moves slowly from the left hand side of the screen to the right.

The 260B is designed for systems operation, and may be
interconnected with audio sources for sequential voice/video

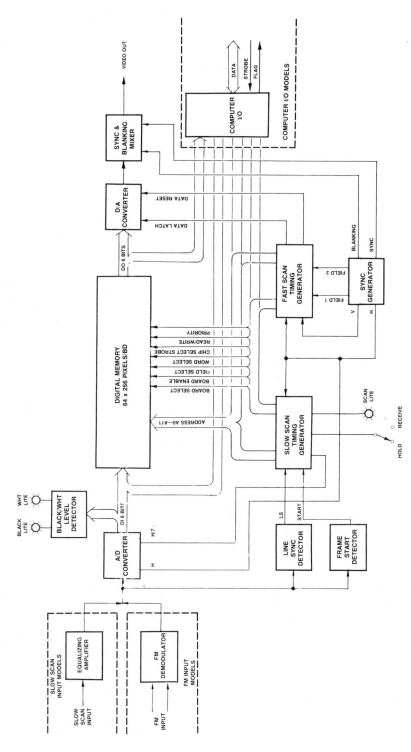

figure 5–14 A simplified block diagram of the CVI 275 video expander.

Courtesy: Colorado Video, Inc.

transmission. Options include operation from 625 line video input sources, and digital transmission at rates of 2,400 bits/ second or higher.

Insofar as compressed video also lends itself to digital transmission, it may be considered a distant relation of facsimile in that both are systems for the transmission of images over telephone circuits. Both transmissions can be analog or digital in nature; but one primarily produces a hard copy, whereas the other yields successive electronic images. Whereas facsimile is characterized by the relatively slow transmission of documents and photographs with high definition, compressed video has a gray scale but lower definition, and a much more flexible "action" image communication format. The TV camera can view microscopic or macroscopic subjects, flat or three dimensional, near or distant, and if required, in color. At the receiving location, pictures are rapidly displayed on one or many monitors or modified standard TV screens with sizes ranging from the 9 inch desk top monitor to large-scale projection for group viewing. Compressed video consumes no paper, and it is relatively free of the mechanical wear problems associated with facsimile.

Vidicom, the distributor for CVI in Hawaii and California, puts out a system that uses standard television monitors to display images. Transmission is again accomplished by compressing the television signals so that they may be sent over telephone lines. At the receiver, the signals are restored to high-resolution television signals or automatically stored on a videodisc recorder for later viewing.

The Vidicom system can transmit any type of image, including CRT displays, engineering drawings, blackboard diagrams, models, or any three-dimensional object. The transmission of a single image can take as little as 35 seconds. In a teleconferencing situation, a separate audio hookup would be in effect so that conversation between the two points could occur simultaneously with video transmission. With computer conferencing combined with fax, the system is called "audiographic."

Whereas CVI's systems are considered primarily "closed circuit," the SSTV systems of Robot Research are considered primarily PLTV. The Robot phone line system is the first slow-scan system offered for a price within the consumer's reach— 212 $1,500. Robot's system converts the video image to an audio

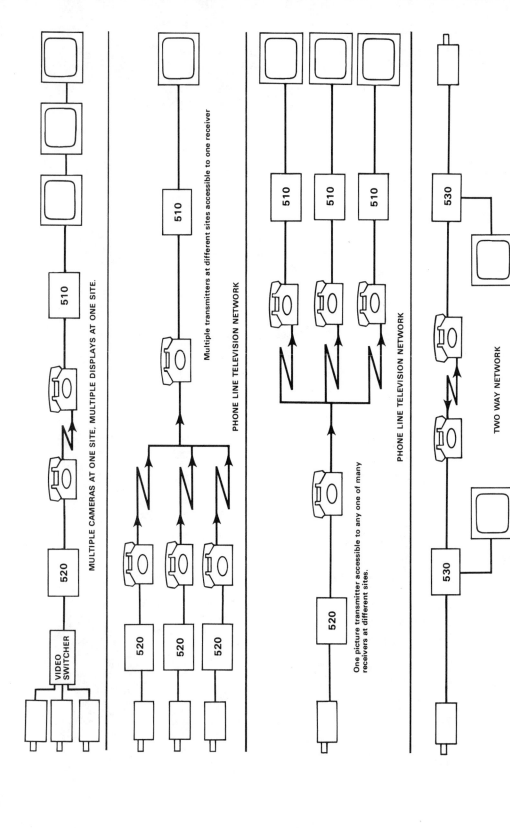

MULTIPLE CAMERAS AT ONE SITE, MULTIPLE DISPLAYS AT ONE SITE.

Multiple transmitters at different sites accessible to one receiver

PHONE LINE TELEVISION NETWORK

One picture transmitter accessible to any one of many receivers at different sites.

PHONE LINE TELEVISION NETWORK

TWO WAY NETWORK

Courtesy: Robot Research, Inc.

figure 5-15   PLTV system.

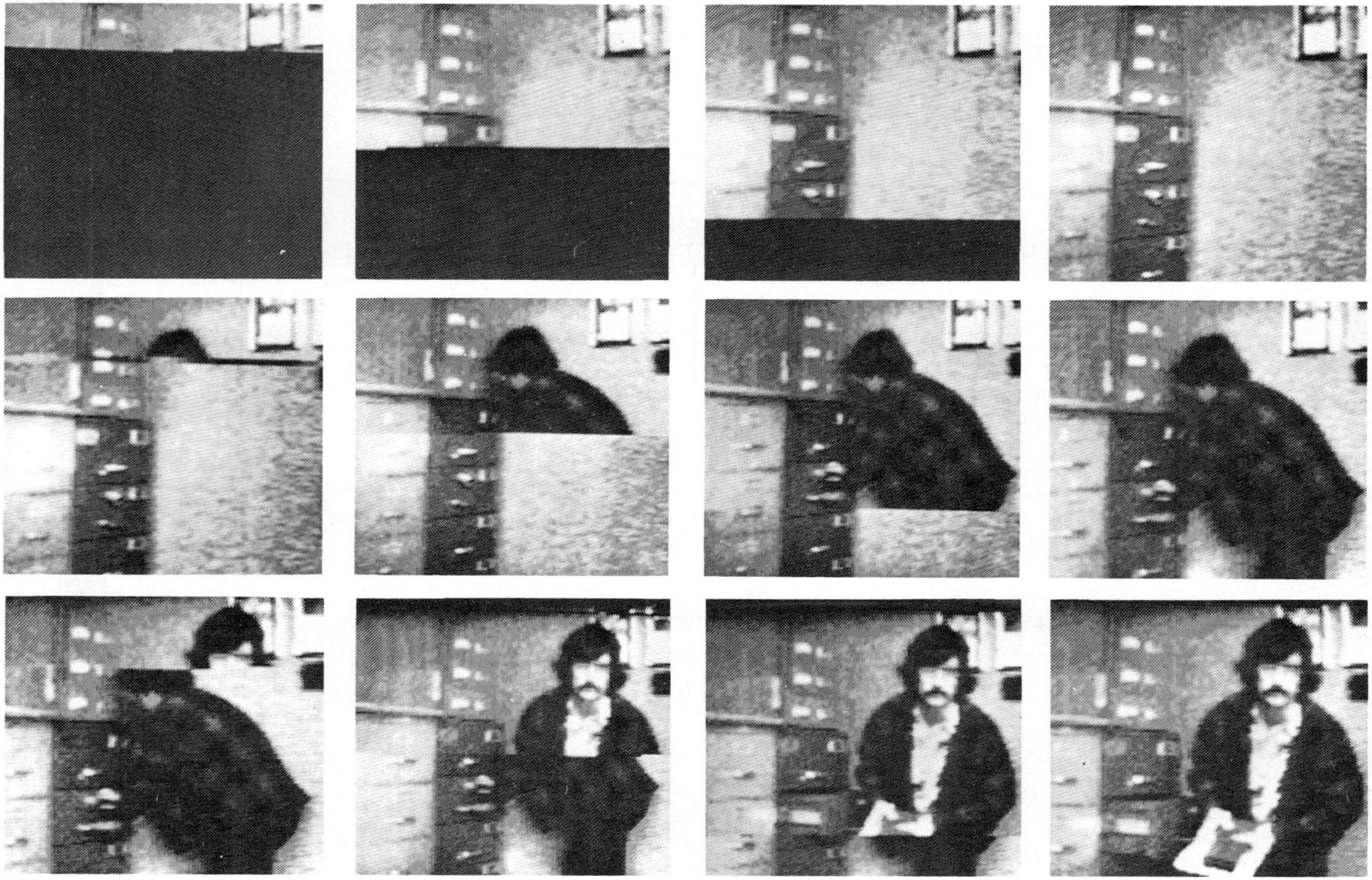

figure 5–16   Motion is displayed as a series of changing pictures.

Courtesy: Robot Research, Inc.

tone especially for transmission over phone lines (Figure 5–15). The trade-off is a picture of diminished quality (Figure 5–16). But improvements were in prototype equipment stages.

The beauty of this type of system is that either is compatible with computer input/output data transmission. SSTV and data communications are both digital in nature, both communicable over phone lines, and both presentable on the same types of screens. Even though it is not a fast-scan picture, some very fine combined graphic presentations could be worked up with an adequate program.

LARGER SYSTEMS VIA PHONE LINES

Nippon Electric Company (NEC) is one of the major companies putting the pieces together in video and computer communications, especially with their telephone video systems (TVS). (See Figure 5–17.) Their freeze-frame transceivers make it possible to video conference on a global scale. Two models are

figure 5–17   NEC's TVS-751 is a solid-state, digital PCM video system developed for an unlimited variety of applications where video images must be transmitted over long distances. The system reflects NEC's breakthroughs in digital and band compression technology to the long-distance transmission of still or "freeze" video images. The TVS-751 can transmit over coaxial cables, telephone wires, microwave systems, or VHF/UHF channels. It will also accept a computer interface for the wide expansion of system capabilities.

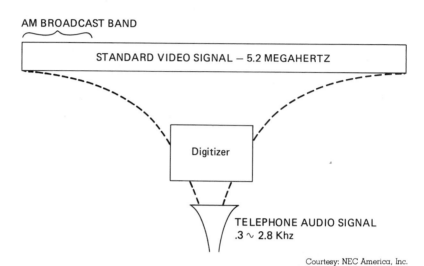

figure 5-18   The TVS-751 compresses the standard video signal into a bandwidth compatible with telephone lines.

available; one for use in black-and-white (TVS-754) and one for color (TVS-751) applications. The equipment takes an incoming video signal (camera, videotape, etc.), captures one full image, digitizes it in a solid-state memory, and translates the picture to data for transmission on phone lines. The reception equipment accepts the data from the phone lines, loads a memory for display, and converts the digital signal back to conventional television images for display on any standard TV monitor. To transmit a complex television signal over narrow telephone channels the picture is stored, separated into discrete elements and transmitted piece by piece at a rate appropriate to the telephone line capability. Transmission times vary according to the line's quality and the signal's complexity (color as opposed to black and white). NEC's black-and-white model works on any standard telephone line and completes a picture transmission in only 30 seconds. The color model changes speed to adjust to differing lines and hookups, so transmission may range from 5 to 300 seconds per picture.

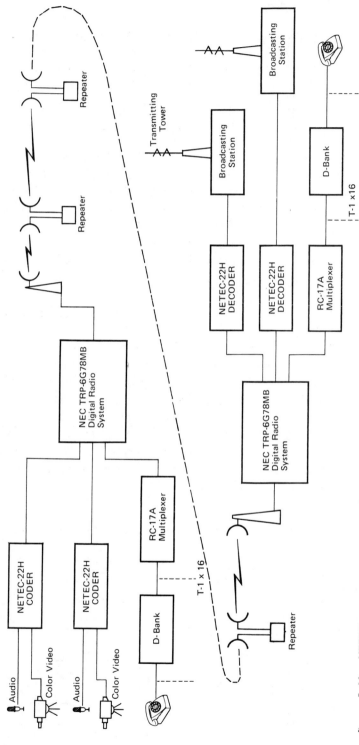

figure 5-19 NETEC on microwave—two NTSC color video signals plus 384 voice channels.

Courtesy: NEC America, Inc.

Unlike the expense of leased video lines or microwave, TVS equipment connects the user for the price of a normal telephone call. A two-day meeting for presentation of a new marketing plan or construction project may be held coast-to-coast for a fraction of the cost of the travel, lodging, and general expenses normally involved—and have the same immediacy. A doctor may analyze X-rays, diagnose, and prescribe to isolated areas otherwise devoid of medical service. Multiple camera plant security systems are easily linked to any point in the world. The communication applications for such systems as the TVS are still being discovered. The availability of the equipment itself will undoubtedly create new applications. In other words, owners of the equipment have the phone lines of the world at their disposal, for only the relatively nominal cost of the equipment.

VIA CONVENTIONAL MEDIA

Other systems by NEC offer even greater capabilities. Their band-compressed digital TV terminal system (called "NETEC" for *NEC Television Encoding* and Bandwidth Compression) is capable of broadcasting digitized information of any kind—video, audio, or data—over just about any medium: microwaves, satellite, cable, or phone lines. When transmitted over anything but phone lines the signal is a high-quality digitized video, audio, and possibly data display. Sent over phone lines, it is freeze-frame (Figure 5–20).

figure 5–20   A typical application layout for the equipment shown in Figure 5–18.

Courtesy: NEC America, Inc.

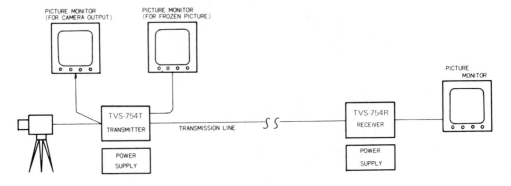

Whether it is an isolated HAM SSTV station in an isolated part of North Dakota or teeming Tokyo, the basic principle of video/computer communications is developing along the same line. The composite signal is digitized and then strung out (compressed) according to the speed of the transmission medium. The differences lie in how the systems are developing and in their degree of sophistication. The overriding point is that video/computer transmissions are becoming more and more feasible all around the world.

The Media

The only inhibiting factor seems to be with the media itself—phone lines, coax, fiber optics, radio bands, TV bands, satellites, everything but two cans and a string! To deal with the cost problem, many experiments are underway, only some of which can be listed here.

Fiber Optics

A new medium that is being widely substituted for coax cable is fiber optics. The cable itself is actually a bundle of hair-thin glass fibers, each of which is capable of carrying light beams. Like coax, it varies in diameter according to its type or application. Also like coax, it handles many kinds of transmission. Unlike coax, its design and installation are not as pat. For example, fiber optics' manufacturers are still dealing with relative unknowns with regard to ambient temperature conditions, water and corrosion sensitivity, the effects of abuse and animal pests, and many other factors. In most instances, they know how the cable *should* hold up, but the empirical results are still coming in. And they *do* know that the ultimate information-bearing capacity of fiber optics is far greater than any existing wire cables.

Nonetheless, fiber optics are noted by many as the fastest growing segment of communications components. Worldwide fiber optic use is expected to increase by one-third each year. By 1990 the value of fiber optics investments in North America alone should exceed a billion dollars a year. An editorial in the

August 1978 issue of *JEE* (*Japan Electronic Engineering* magazine) stated:

> Optical data processing systems utilizing lasers are emerging from their infancy and may eventually end up as optical microcomputers or minicomputers.

Quantum Science Corporation, in a study on Worldwide Technology Impact on Information Systems and Services, predicts that fiber optic systems will be commonly used for broadband distribution of data, graphic material, and electronic mail by 1982.

The full potential of fiber optics is yet to be tapped. For example, in June of 1978, Canstar demonstrated a two-way television and computer transmission on a single optical fiber (not a single cable, but a single fiber). This demonstration proved, for the first time, the feasibility and ease of operating teleconferencing *and* computer applications on a single glass fiber. The system transmits video information at 5 mHz in one

figure 5–21   A typical fiber optic cable (this one from Canstar) employs a sheathed central member, surrounded by concentric layers of fibers in individual buffer tubes. These tubes are in turn overlaid with multiple layers of tapes, fillers, fibrous materials, and jackets.

Courtesy:
Canstar Corporation

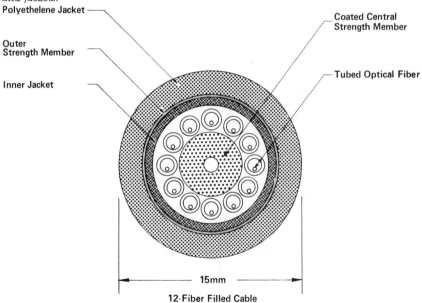

Polyethelene Jacket

Coated Central
Strength Member

Outer
Strength Member

Tubed Optical Fiber

Inner Jacket

15mm

12-Fiber Filled Cable

Courtesy:
Canstar Corporation

figure 5–22 Canstar also produces fiber optic modems, with the options of feeding a single transmission to multiple receivers or of operating on a full-duplex basis. The quality of the transmission is, of course, dependent on the length of the cable used.

direction and computer data at up to 2 megabits per second in the other direction. Similar systems will be used for mixed video and computer data transmissions in automated offices and in computerized industrial control systems of the future. Two-way transmission on the single fiber is made possible by the recently announced Canstar multiport coupler, which can be used to feed signals from different sources in and out of a single fiber. It also allows the attachment of a number of computer network configurations.

The cable, one of many by Canstar, is easily installed. Less than a ¼″ in diameter, the cable can be installed in ducts or simply routed under a carpet or along baseboards in an office. The use of fiber optics cable eliminates static electricity and other forms of electrical interference often found in an office or industrial environment.

Fiber optics promise to be *the* future "wire" medium, especially at first for localized video/computer networks—say with a building complex, a school system, or enterprising community. However, phone lines, coax, and fiber optics cannot be brought everywhere, certainly not for a long while.

Satellites

Although only a half-dozen or so American companies are able to build communications satellites—Hughes Aircraft Co., TRW, Inc., RCA, and a few others—this situation is changing rapidly as Japanese and European countries are not about to live with a U.S. monopoly. By the end of 1979, when AT&T-GTE's Comstar satellite systems for private-line use went into use (after a three-year moratorium imposed by the Federal Communications Commission to allow others to get a "good start" before the fight), the U.S. had more than doubled its transponders from 72 in July, 1979 to 180 in December, 1979. RCA and Western Union were each launching their fifth by 1982, but more were approved in early 1981.

RCA and WU were evidently doing a land-office business with cable-TV systems and noncable entertainment companies offering pay-TV using satellites and telephone and other company microwave systems. "Supertelevision" and "superradio" stations, as well as the Public Broadcast System (PBS), were making "gold rush" progress signing up customers all over the U.S. The proliferation of birds was expected to spark many more imaginative remote TV offerings and uses—well beyond sporting, entertainment, and news events. Direct access to satellites for TV viewing was growing in Japan and West Germany, and nothing was going to stop it in the U.S. as earth antennas fell to the $1,000-and-below ranges. Scientific Atlanta, Inc. was only one of dozens of companies pushing hard in the earth stations business, with some Japanese firms already leading.

Satellites at first were expected to merely complement ground-bound communications networks wherever network construction fell short or got too expensive, such as in rural areas, undeveloped countries or transoceanic situations. Also, satellites were expected to be used only in the "big league ballparks," that is, by IBM, AT&T, Xerox, RCA, Western Union, and other industrial giants. Now the cost of launching and positioning a satellite has been reduced to the point that even small groups of enthusiasts can either benefit from more numerous existing satellites or launch their own. Satellites are extremely feasible cost-effective media for even personal video/computer enthusiasts now and in the near future.

222

After Russia shocked American scientists into the race for space with the launching of "Sputnik" on October 10, 1957, the United States started sending up one satellite after another. In 1958, Vanguard and Explorer went up and then down again, which merely demonstrated that we could achieve an orbit. Later in 1958, the U.S. launched Score, which broadcast a tape recorded Christmas message from President Eisenhower to the world. Two years later saw the launching of Echo, a 100-foot diameter balloon whose surface was composed of metalized plastic that reflected radio waves. Echo was big enough and low enough in its orbit to be seen easily with the naked eye. Also in 1960, NASA and Philco-Ford (Ford Aerospace Communications Corporation) launched Courier—the first communications satellite. It received messages from earth; a tape recorder on board later played back and retransmitted these messages to earth.

None of these satellites could receive signals and retransmit them back to earth in real time until TELSTAR was launched in 1962. TELSTAR contained communications equipment that served as an active repeater; it could receive, amplify, and retransmit messages in real time. This type of equipment is known as a *transponder*. Signals from earth are received by the satellite, their frequency is changed, and they are amplified and retransmitted back to earth.

These early satellites were put into what is known as a low orbit. Their period of revolution around the earth is less than 24 hours. Usually their plane of the orbit does not lie in the plane of the equator, either. Although the orbits maximized the satellites' visibility from the ground, the antennas on the ground had to be capable of continuously tracking their positions. Yet communication was periodically lost as the satellite passed over the horizon.

Meanwhile, the U.S. government, acting with unusual speed and unanimity of purpose, formed the Communications Satellite Corporation, known as COMSAT, by an Act of Congress in 1962. An international agreement had been signed in the previous year to form the International Telecommunications Satellite Organization, or Intelsat, to provide international service.

Comsat has served as technical manager of Intelsat from
223

the beginning. In 1965, Intelsat I was launched. This satellite was larger and more powerful than the Syncom, drawing power from its solar cells; it could transmit 240 voice channels or one TV channel. The Intelstat organization now has 95 member nations and over 100 earth station locations throughout the world. Most of these earth stations are very large, having antenna diameters of 30 meters (97 feet).

Over the next decade, Intelsat introduced four generations of spacecraft, or "spinners," so named because they spin like tops about their axis of symmetry to maintain stability. The antenna system however, does not spin so that it can point continuously to a specified location on earth. Until 1975, the U.S. and USSR were the only countries capable of putting payloads into synchronous orbit. Then both France and Japan built rockets capable of launching modest payloads.

The sixth and final Intelsat IV-A communications satellite by Hughes Aircraft joined its sister vehicles in synchronous orbit 22,300 miles above the Equator in late 1978. This last satellite in the Intelsat IV-A series, placed into orbit over the Indian Ocean, provides services to over 40 countries. Technological advances over the years have reduced the cost of satellite transmission considerably. For example, the cost of TV transmission had fallen from $22,000 to $5,000 per hour and was even lower in 1980.

In the early days, earth stations were very large and complex, exactly the opposite of the early satellites, which were small, simple, and relatively unsophisticated. Not until the development of NASA's ATS-6, launched in 1974, was the burden of performance transferred from the earth stations to the satellite.

The first step in keeping closer track of these satellites was to fix them in one spot in a space. First the orbit had to be *synchronous;* that is, the rotation of the satellite about the earth must be exactly synchronized with the earth's own revolution. If a satellite's orbital plane lies in the plane of the equator, the satellite spends half its time in the Northern Hemisphere and half in the Southern Hemisphere bobbing up and down in the sky. Since synchronous satellites with equatorial orbits appear stationary to an observer on earth, they are called geostationary satellites. The first spacecraft to achieve a geostationary synchronous orbit was the Syncom I, built by Hughes Aircraft and launched by NASA in 1963. A technical triumph, Syncom was the basis for design for the next 10 years. Syncom had one transponder which was capable of relaying either one TV channel or 50 telephone circuits.

In spinners, the predominant type of communication satellites in the late seventies, the upper section always points toward its target station on earth, while the lower section spins to provide the necessary momentum for stability. Recently, body-stabilized or three-axis, satellites have been successfully launched, beginning with NASA's Applications Technology Satellite # 6 (ATS-6). NASA's ATS program stimulated continued development and innovation. The ATS-1 and ATS-3, widely known for their voice communications services at VHF in Alaska and throughout the western hemisphere, were conceived in the early sixties and launched in 1966 and 1967, respectively. After many difficulties, ATF-6 proved to be successful both in advancing space technology as well as in demonstrating the utility of communication satellites to public service.

ATS-6 achieved many firsts, the most relevant being the first highpowered transmitter. The transmitter, which operates at 860 mHz and 2500 mHz, permits use of relatively small, simple earth stations. Successful demonstrations of the technology occurred in the U.S. and in India. Nontechnical laypersons can definitely operate and maintain the earth stations. ATF-6 has therefore heralded transition to communications networks in which the performance burden is placed on the satellite rather than on the earth station.

The current operational communication satellite systems are used to provide trunk telephony service to common carriers, video distribution service to organizations such as Home Box Office, and occasional private-line point-to-point voice or data communications. For most of these applications, the antenna "footprints" (antenna coverage) has to provide coverage to continent, including Alaska and the U.S. offshore islands, such as Puerto Rico and Hawaii. New applications may require completely different antenna coverage patterns.

Spot beams will increase the capacity for new applications. Spot beams may be of future use if enough become available, but the relatively small geographic coverage limits the usefulness to experimental programs. Presently available technology makes it possible to deploy a full range of telecommunications 225

figure 5–23 Applications Technology Satellite (ATS-6) is designed and built for NASA by Fairchild Space and Electronics Company.

services on the same satellite, from the long-haul telephone trunking services to distribution satellites and community broadcasting satellites.

Future uses definitely include widespread video distribution, with limited interactive feedback links, emergency mobile services, and rural telephony interconnections. Expediting the more widespread use of satellites is the possibility of launching large spacecrafts via the space shuttle. The costs for a shuttle launch are far lower than for a launch by an expendable rocket. The capacity of the shuttle is also significantly higher than any of the presently used rockets, except for the Saturn.

Spacecraft designers will no longer be constrained to deploy satellites having a size and weight to fit, for example, the Thor Delta family of launchers.

Public service users must now create a system that can put all this technology to effective use. And they seem to be going about the job in two ways:

1. public satellites are being launched, and
2. small, low-cost, and easy-to-use earth stations are being created.

PUBLIC SATELLITES

An affordable, wide-band, high-speed communications medium is too good an opportunity to pass up, especially by video/computers. Satellites can accept and pass on broadband information of the type needed for fast-scan, full-color, PCM audio, and data transmissions. As the price of a satellite launch drops, the feasibility of a small organization putting up a satellite increases.

RCA.   RCA American Communications originally planned to have only one or two satellites. By November of 1981, however, the company had launched its fourth, and it had received permission from the FCC to launch a fifth satellite—just to meet increasing demand.

SBS.   Satellite Business Systems (SBS) is a subsidiary of International Business Machines (IBM), Comsat, and Aetna. The SBS network skirts the bandwidth-limited local loops operated by AT&T and the independent telephone companies by installing satellite earth stations on the roof tops or parking lots of the nations' major businesses. High-speed computer-to-computer data transmission, high-volume electronic mail, teleconferencing to replace costly travel, and high-quality voice conversations are the principal applications.

The SBS system will be innovative, flexible, and technologically advanced. It will be the first commercial system to include these important technological features:

1. small earth stations sited on customer premises,
2. integrated voice data image communications in a digital format,   227

figure 5–24 The first Satellite Business Systems (SBS) spacecraft was delivered by Hughes Aircraft Company in 1980, with two others following at three-month intervals.

3. time-division, multiple access (TDMA) techniques with demand assignment (DA), and

4. utilization of the 12 and 14 gHz bands of the frequency spectrum.

Two SBS spacecrafts were scheduled for launch in the latter half of 1980 for the SBS Operational System, which will be in service in January 1981. The two-satellite configuration will provide complete in-orbit redundancy, and a ground spare will be available for launch, should it be needed. The satellites will be positioned over the equator, south of the continental United States, at the synchronous altitude of 22,300 miles where they will remain stationary in relation to the earth below. The SBS satellites are designed for 7-year lifetimes in orbit. Each will weigh about 2,400 pounds at injection to transfer orbit. They are designed for launch by NASA's Space Transportation System (the Shuttle) or by a Delta 3910 launch vehicle.

The small earth stations sited on customer premises will bring the SBS network service directly where it is needed. Unlike existing commercial communications satellite systems, which operate in the 4 and 6 gHz bands of the frequency spectrum, the SBS system will operate in the 12 and 14 gHz bands.

The system uses a communications band that had never been proved in practice. While prior satellite networks used the 4 or 6 gHz region. SBS uses the 11/14-gHz region. It thus allows for smaller earth stations. Its disadvantage is that severe weather, such as the waves severly attenuate Comsat Laboratories estimates that SBS operates with degraded service for an average of 44 hours yearly, compared to a standard maxium of 20 hours set by the Intelsat network.

The system is all-digital. Digital systems have improved reliability and quality, but they require greater bandwidth. Implementing an all-digital SBS type network is more expensive than an analog network, particularly to provide a primarily voice-oriented communications mix. The SBS system, however, provides so much bandwidth that the cost of digitizing voice is minimized. SBS can afford to use the 32,000 bps needed for a single digitized voice channel. A terrestrial system would be sorely pressed to provide such a bandwidth.

SBS is economically, as well as technologically, motivated.   *229*

Its owners believe they can garner as much as $1 billion in yearly revenue within 10 years of implementation.

In the process, they would alter the primary method in which major businesses communicate. In so doing, SBS has to convince a cynical user public that its system is really viable. It is an integrated communications network capable of communication feats that cannot be performed by ground systems. Computers, video equipment, audio devices or fax can all be interconnected on a global scale at low cost.

ASC. Another effort to match up lower-budgeted users with satellite communications is the American Satellite Corporation (ASC), a domestic communications satellite common carrier authorized by the FCC to provide satellite communications service within the United States (Figure 5–24). As of 1980, it was also part of a consortium with Continental Telephone, Fairchild Industries, and Western Union. It commenced operations in July

figure 5–25   An American Satellite major commercial earth station near Los Angeles.

Courtesy:
American
Satellite Corporation

figure 5–26 A small 15′ diameter antenna can be placed on a user's rooftop to directly link facilities via satellite.

of 1974. Connections to overseas points are provided in conjunction with International Record Carriers (RCs). American Satellite circuits may be used to transmit voice, data, facsimile, and video.

Various digital communications services, developed by American Satellite are combined in a major service offering, called Satellite Data Exchange (SDX™). (See Figure 5–22.) Under this umbrella, American Satellite can provide all-digital services for voice, data, and facsimile.

New innovations, which are or will be offered as part of the SDX service, include small earth stations that can be placed adjacent to the users' facilities or on the rooftops. Also offered is equipment that allows the user to easily change the mix of communication service, a data encryption device which will assure privacy of the information transmitted and equipment that greatly reduces the effects of data transmission delay.

XTEN. In 1978, Xerox filed a petition with the Federal Communications Commission in November that could lead to the creation of nation-wide common-carrier electronic message services. The company asked the FCC to allocate a band of radio frequencies for document distribution, teleconferencing, and data transmission—the Xerox Telecommunications Network (XTEN). Due to the wide bandwidth of the frequencies requested (10.55–10.68), high-quality graphics could be transmitted at speeds considerably greater than that of current facsimile systems, along with voice transmission, for teleconferences. Xerox would use leased satellite capacity for long-distance transmission of radio signals, which would go from the satellite to ground stations constructed by Xerox.

What are the effects of such a system? Xerox had decided that the present analog telephone systems were too expensive, too cumbersome, and too badly designed to assist in developing the various "offices of the future." The Xerox system would use proven cellular radio techniques to overcome the problems of local networks (loops), which Satellite Business Systems (IBM, Aetna, Comsat) could not. In essence, XTEN is primarily a local

figure 5–27   XTEN switched service.   Courtesy: Xerox Corporation

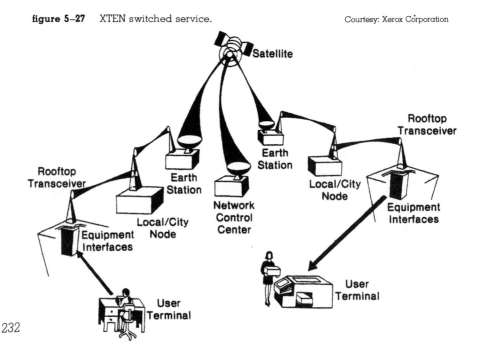

232

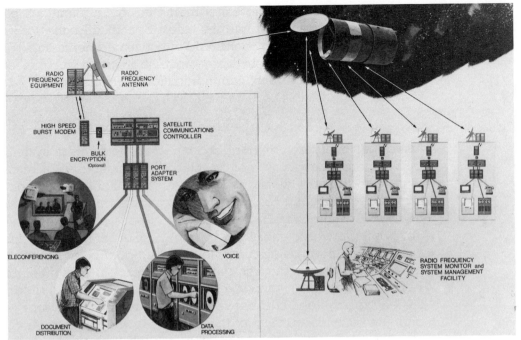

figure 5–28 The Satellite Business System will operate in the 12- and 14-gHz bands, offering private networks with the full range of intercompany communications.

Courtesy: Satellite Business Systems

(secondarily a national) high-speed digital network that is dedicated to communicating business information coded text for computer data, digital facsimile, and other services. The services are aimed primarily at the more than 100,000 U.S. businesses with assets of $1 to $10 million. Very similar to the one operated by American Satellite, XTEN was planned to have far wider development beginning in 1982, to bypass the telephone lines by using rooftop antennas, to offer savings of up to 40 percent and more, to provide freeze frame video, to use a "black box" to compensate for the delay in satellite signals.

PSSC. The Public Service Satellite Consortium (PSCC) is an organization of over 90 nonprofit public service agencies from education, health care, library service, public broadcasting, state government and related interests. Created in 1975, the PSCC detects problems and opportunities in the public service, while exerting pressure when necessary to bring about solutions to public problems. In so doing the consortium moves valid, otherwise ignored, public experiments in communications off the drawing boards and into the skies. Specifically, the PSSC is working with NASA to coordinate public experiments on ATS-6. They should get their way, since there is a surplus of transmission time on most communications satellites today.

CHEAPER EARTH STATIONS

Just about every commercial communications satellite system today offers a low-cost user-oriented earth station. Typical of many efforts in the works now is Hughes' $1,000 earth station. Hughes Aircraft Co.'s Electron Dynamics Division was awarded a $146,000 contract by NASA's Goddard Space Flight Center to develop a low-cost, mass-producible 12-gHz receiver-only for TV reception from broadcast satellites. The goal is to make the receivers available for less than $1,000 each in quantities of 1,000. Current earth stations, 4½ to 5 meters in diameter, are in the 4-gHz range and cost between $20,000 and $30,000. Hughes attributes a major portion of the expense to the large antenna and complex installation. The new models, which won't be commercially available until the mid or late 1980s, could be as small as 1-meter in diameter.

figure 5–29 An artist's rendering of a 5.5-meter antenna on a customer's rooftop.

Courtesy: Satellite Business Systems

Such stations, however, could lock IVTs into satellite, rather than into earth-bound, communications, if they became available soon enough. The reason is that an end user, individual or not, can buy and use a station receiver a lot more easily than laying optic fiber to wherever transmissions must be sent.

Summary

One conclusion, which has both its happy and unfortunate elements, is that communication media of all kinds are going digital. Phone, cable, optical fiber, short-wave, UHF/VHF, and others all seem to derive benefits from converting the signal to digital form before transmission. This tendency presents the video/computer enthusiasts with a dilemma. With an integrated terminal with components that are both analog and digital in nature, the analog system is the more practical one for fast-scan video. Digitizing devices for video output only hold up the computer components so that they become "video-bound." On the other hand, just about every communications medium is set up to accept digital input. Hence the oddest part of the whole IVT concept.

chapter **6**

Conclusion

So many new gadgets, new ideas, new techniques, new power, and new possibilities . . . so much has been thrust upon us in the last few years that few of us can sort out what's happening. This "confusion syndrome" often holds as much for the professional as it does for the paraprofessional or hobbyist—not to mention the more casual, nontechnical user. As we all stand amazed, manufacturers keep throwing more and more gizmos on the technological heap with each passing year. Annual conventions are becoming, more and more, an exhibition of sophisticated electronic Rube Goldberg devices.

Some things, however, are pretty clear. For one thing, everyone is watching the digital trend with great interest. The emergence of a digitizer with a high enough speed to give us fast-scan video images is just the "shot" that the IVT needs to become the universal hardware it is destined to be. In the communications area, receive-only individual satellites for under $1,000 hold out a promise of digital communications via satellite *for individuals!* With such a development, home computerists could easily slip free from the entanglement of phone lines and cables that is presently holding up unlimited, economical, digital communication among personal computer users.

At the very least, most of us have the basis for the type of terminal that is undoubtedly the home "desk" of the future. As the 1978 report of International Resource Development, Inc., on the *Home Terminal* stated:

> The services converge in the home. The home itself is the only site at which effective convergence of these competing, regulated, and legally separated services can take place.
>
> The home terminal is the place where innovation, integration, and synergistic services will originate. It is the *only* place where the law will permit it to happen.

So while it would have been easy to get carried away with exciting peripheral equipment that would hang like decorations on a tree, we have tried to bear down on issues, on essential problems, on the difficulties—not the easy parts—of selecting, mixing, and operating such a system.

By the end of the 1980's, the integrated video terminal, in one form or another, is destined to assume a central role in the home, in the office, and in all areas of our lives. That is the central issue. If in the meanwhile we encounter momentary delays due to pricing, technology, or some sort of legality, we really should consider them steppingstones. No doubt, for instance, before long the A/D conversion process will speed up to the point that a digital IVT system will become not only feasible, but also desirable and necessary. And the miasma currently surrounding the bog of muckish legalities and entangled media is sure to be resolved, as more and more individuals impress government and business alike of their need for faster, cheaper, more accurate means of communication. At that time, the fully integrated video terminal will become an essential part of a worldwide network of *total* communications.

Index

245